Savanah Boike lives in a small town in Southwest Minnesota. In her spare time, she likes to spend time with her husband, Mitchel, and playing with her dogs, Kale and Sammi. She also enjoys going to the gym, where she is learning kickboxing and continues to journal and write poetry.

To Mitchel, my wonderful and faithful husband.

Savanah Boike

I'M OK

My Journey Through Schizophrenia

AUSTIN MACAULEY PUBLISHERS™

LONDON ∗ CAMBRIDGE ∗ NEW YORK ∗ SHARJAH

Ordering Information
Quantity sales: Special discounts are available on quantity purchases by corporations, associations, and others. For details, contact the publisher at the address below.

Publisher's Cataloging-in-Publication data
Boike, Savanah
I'm OK

ISBN 9781649790088 (Paperback)
ISBN 9781649790125 (Hardback)
ISBN 9781649790132 (ePub e-book)

Library of Congress Control Number: 2021919373

www.austinmacauley.com/us

First Published 2021
Austin Macauley Publishers LLC
40 Wall Street, 33rd Floor, Suite 3302
New York, NY 10005
USA

mail-usa@austinmacauley.com
+1 (646) 5125767

Mitchel, I would've never made it to where I am now without your love and support. You have been there through all ups and downs, and never stopped looking for new ways to help me understand my illness. You could have gone, but you stayed. I still remember what you said to me about loving me and that you remember who I am even when I am sick. I also want to thank you for the amount of time and effort you put into our relationship.

Thanks to my support system who has always answered my calls when I am in need. The people who were there for me at night while I was alone, and coming over to sit with me. Being there to give me faith and a sense of security, knowing I am OK and safe.

To the many hospitals and facilities I have stayed at, I want to thank them anonymously for their support and encouragement when I was too ill to function. Some doctors were better than others but they all had the same objective, and that was to get me well enough to function with daily life.

Table of Contents

Prologue

Savanah,

It's been a long time since you have been back. I am proud of you for working so hard to become better. There are things you need to know for the next time you start slipping up. You need to remember how good your progress can be. You need to realize that the voices you hear are lying to you and the paranoid delusions are not real. I know it's hard in the state of mind you are in right now but I'm telling you it will pass. You are worth the fight so do not give up even though you relapse. I want you to know that it isn't a bad thing to reach out or get help. The main thing to know is that when you start to go under and someone wants to take you to the hospital or crisis facility... GO! They are stepping in before you go deep down before you can't get out. The support system you have built are full of people who are on your side and is in the best interest of you. Listen. Do not deny but try to realize that you are sick. I know you don't like that word but it is true and you need to understand. Advice to you: when you begin to get paranoid, try to understand that it's just your brain and not who you are as a person. You are deeper than this. You can fight and overcome like you have done so far. The visual hallucinations frightening at the time will pass. They will live in your memories forever but not so constant at the time. The auditory hallucinations you hear are scary as well but they won't hurt you. You need to overpower the voices with your own thoughts and speak out the truth not what they are saying. Do not believe them! They are not telling you the truth. They are liars. Remember who you are. You are a strong woman who has come so far in your journey.

—Your healthy self

Timeline of My Illness

Aug. 2013- Started College

Oct. 2nd 2013- First diagnosis of Bipolar and Borderline Personality Disorder

During this time I was started on Latuda which was really expensive

Feb. 2014- First Hospitalization- hospitalized for mood dysregulation and homicidal ideation.

2014- Met with new doctor Deb- Latuda, Seroquel, Lamictal

soon changed to Geodon instead of Latuda due to price.

The Dark Figures first appeared in spring of 2015- mentioned at 3/10/2017

Spring 2015- I met with a new doctor, Dr. Mag, and she prescribed me Paliperidone, Seroquel and Lamictal.

May 16th 2015- Married Mitchel :)

June/July 2016- 1st hospitalization at New Ulm- Changed to Risperidone

December 2016- Still not functioning so we try Vraylar, a new medication.

March 22nd 2017- 2nd hospitalization at New Ulm- Began Haldol- Diagnosis Schizoaffective Bipolar Type

April 2017- Increased Haldol

Light Bringers came to help in the fight against the evil ones

Invisible People made their presence known- June of 2017

August 2017- 3rd hospitalization at New Ulm- Zyprexa, Haldol, and Seroquel

Therapist Diagnostic Assessment - Paranoid Schizophrenia

January 2018 & May 22nd 2018- The Beast

January 2018- Began college but soon had to stay at the Crisis Facility

February 2018- Austin Hospital- discontinued Seroquel and Haldol- stayed on Zyprexa and Lamictal

March 15th 2018- April 9th 2018- 2nd Hospitalization at Austin- DIAGNOSIS CONFIRMED

April 9th - July 13th 2018- I stayed at an IRTS facility where my medications were changed from Zyprexa, Clozaril, and Haldol.

May 18th 2018- Delusion of Computer Man

May 18th 2018- The War to Come

June 2018- The delusion of the Checkpoint

May 2018- The idea of the Red Button being in a facility to stop the computer man

August 2018- 500mg Clozaril, 20mg Zyprexa (decreased), Haldol

September 25th 2018- 30mg Abilify, 400mg Clozaril and .5mg Klonopin (PRN)

October 31st 2018- Help Line go to ER

December 5th 2018- The idea of an army taking control to aid in the war to come

November 1st - Nov. 5th Sioux Falls Hospital- Clozaril, Saphris and Lamictal

February 2019- Sioux Falls Hosp. - 20mg Haldol (didn't work) - Saphris, Clozaril, and Lamictal (the same as admission)

March 2019- I convinced my doctor to let me discontinue the Clozaril but had to taper down slowly

July 23rd 2019- This was the night I was completely off of Clozaril - I began to become symptomatic again

August 12th 2019- August 18th 2019- I was admitted to the Crisis Facility

August 19th 2019- Albert Lea - possible commitment

August 30th 2019- Called help line referred me to ER

August 30th 2019- Went to ER and was transferred to Owatonna Hospital

September 6th 2019- Left Owatonna and now home

Chapter One
Growing Up

When I was just a girl, I learned how cruel the world could be. My parents divorced when I was just seven years old. We were what I thought a happy family, but soon I discovered the truth. I have two older brothers who enjoyed BMX racing. I followed suit when I was this age. I remember my dad holding my bike between his legs to help balance me at the gate before it would drop. We lived in Sand Springs, Oklahoma, just outside of Tulsa.

After my parents divorced in Oklahoma, my mom lived in a house and my dad was living in his car. What I remember most was my dad had to scrounge up money by saving what he could so he could reserve a hotel room for the weekend, so we could visit him. Since he was living in his car, he had to provide a place to stay for visitation. He didn't have a lot of money, so we would go to the gas station and get sandwich meat and bread for our meal. At the gas station my dad told me to grab mayonnaise packets to which I asked, "Isn't that stealing?"

My dad said, "No, they want you to take them."

My dad soon was offered a place to stay at our friends, Sam and Paula's. He stayed in a heated shed there that was furnished with a bed. He had a plaid quilt which we named the 'homeless blanket'. I was always a bit wary about going to this place because Sam and Paula had a big dog named Boots. When we would stay at my dad's, we played games like charades and would have fun inside Sam and Paula's house where their son would play card games with me.

My dad was a kind man with a gentle smile. He had a sense of humor that could turn your bad day into a good one. He would always know what to say to make you feel reassured and always gave me great advice. It wasn't until I was older that I realized how much we had in common. I also felt like I was the stranger in the family only related by blood. One thing that I enjoyed was spending time with him snuggling with him in the recliner. I continued to do this even as a teenager. It was a safe spot.

A few years later, my dad got a job in Windom, MN at a rendering plant so as a family we moved. Mom and Dad agreed to try again so we could be together. My dad came up first and secured a house we called the 'farmhouse'. At the farmhouse, we had acres of land that we explored with our English bulldog, Tank. Since we lived in the country, my family suggested us to get ducks for pets. My duck was named Duckie. Sadly, one night there was a commotion outside. I could hear the ducks loudly quacking and honking in their coop. My dad said that they were OK but then the next day we found that one of the ducks had been killed by an unknown animal.

When we first moved to Windom, I was nine and I wasn't sure about making friends in a new school. I soon found myself meeting my best friend, Tanisha. We would have many slumber parties and I was often the first one she would invite to her parties. I got her a purple bunny rabbit for her present. She was a sweet girl whose life would soon mimic my own.

My family was living together at the farmhouse, but there was always fighting. At the house I would sit behind the garbage can and watch my parents yell at one another and my mom would throw things. I was always nervous because I didn't know how far the fights would go. Sometimes I would stand in the middle of them and tell them to stop. There wasn't any happiness within our home, and it is something I desperately wanted. After trying to be together for us kids, my parents lived apart in separate houses. My mom moved into a house on 9th St. and my dad moved into what we called the 'train' house. We called it the train house because it was made out of two train cars.

After the split my mom and dad had joint custody but soon my brothers decided to leave and live with my dad because they were treated poorly. My mom gave up my brothers, but I was stuck with visitation on the weekends because she had sole custody of me. When my brothers moved out, they left some things behind which I then put on my dresser and made a 'shrine' of them. I missed them so much, but I knew I would see them at school and on the weekends.

The good times with my brothers were spent playing CSI or spies. One Christmas at my mom's, I received a play kitchen set. We set it up and soon tore it down while having a plastic food fight. It was my bother Jon and me versus Charlie. It was fun but short-lived as they had to leave to go back to my dad's.

The weekends with my dad were filled with fun, joy and love. The holidays were the best, not because we got presents but it was a time that the whole family could be together. At Christmas my brothers would usually get a new video game. I wanted to play but I usually watched instead, and I was content with this.

Christmas was short at my mom's because I would go to my dad's after supper and presents. Although it was short, my mother and I enjoyed having time together having 'coffee parties' with my tea set. We also liked to play restaurant when I once made Hawaiian surprise which was toast with peanut butter, chocolate syrup, and sugar. She pretended to eat it and like it.

In elementary school, I began to bring my Bible to school and preach to the other students to help save other students. I felt like it was my duty to witness to these kids and make sure that they were saved with Jesus in their heart.

The kids at school thought I was weird and when I entered fifth grade, I lost all my friends except Tanisha. In fifth grade, Tanisha's parents got divorced and she moved away to Illinois. At this point I was only seeing her during the summers.

Each summer came with the excitement of us being able to see each other. We would go to the pool together, clean my house, and watch 'A Haunting', a ghost television show. As the summer came to an end, it was bittersweet. We would meet each other at the end of the street by my house only having the streetlamp to light our goodbyes. We would hug each other and cry because we were never sure if she would be back the next year.

At our goodbyes, we would give each other a hand-written letter that always said, "read after I leave."

I am not sure why but because of my home life, I began to slip into deep depression. At this time, my mom had met my now stepdad, Darren. I felt like I was being replaced as one night I had a nightmare and when I went into my mom's room for safety, I found Darren sleeping in my spot in the bed. I was about twelve when we moved into his house.

One weekend, when my mom and Darren came to pick me up from my dad's, they had a surprise for me. I didn't see it at first and threw my basketball into the vehicle. When I climbed in the truck, I found myself face to face with a petite Yorkie-poo with a pink bow in her hair. Her name was Jazmine and she would become my best friend. I taught her to 'mush', like the dogs in the Iditarod race in Alaska, when I would shake the leash, she would run.

Shortly after we moved in, they got married and my little brother Gunnar was born. A few years later, they had my youngest brother, Liam. I was happy to be a big sister but soon I found myself becoming their caretaker by babysitting them most of the time. The years with my little brothers were a bit estranged because of the age difference. Gunnar and I had more time together than Liam and me. I remember when I would be home with Gunnar, we would watch the same *Thomas the Train* movie. It was annoying, and I can still hear the song in my head going 'boo boo choo choo'. When he was a toddler and needed to nap, I would lay with him and close my eyes, so he would follow me and fall asleep. I remember that he liked to get into my makeup and steal my blush brush and run around the house with it while I chased him. He giggled and thought it was hilarious.

I was in the sixth grade when I made the choice to cut my hair and dress in all black to try to express the deep hate I felt for the people I had to deal with daily. I was a little bottle of rage. Holding onto any wrongdoing, letting it stew for a long time until I would explode. I would take my anger out on people who were closest to me like my mom.

This brings me to the time I had an altercation with another student. He was making fun of my brothers calling them 'gay'. I told him to stop but he wouldn't and continued with it. I told him I would see him in sixth hour which was gym. At gym time, I went up to the student who was making fun of my brothers and put my hands around his throat. My teacher saw and called the principal down to visit with me. I was then sent to Rainbow Behavioral Center for anger management. I wasn't sure what they wanted with me, but they had me draw pictures of things I liked to do.

After the counseling sessions, I didn't feel any better but became filled with rage toward my family and classmates. I started to be bullied when I had the drastic change in appearance and mindset. They also would tell me to go kill myself and to go in a corner and cut myself. I wanted to switch schools and go to Mountain Lake Public School, but my mom said no because of the route she had to take for work, and she couldn't afford to send me to Mountain Lake Christian School. It wasn't until seventh grade that I took their advice and began to self-harm.

When I began to cut, I used one of our large kitchen knives but soon switched to razor blades one of my friends gave me. I kept them in a sock in my dresser drawer. After I would cut, I would wash the razor blade and put ointment on my arms to keep the germs out. I guess you could say that I was a 'good' cutter. Although I did cut, I also began to burn myself with my hair straightener to make it less noticeable. I was still in a deep depression with relentless thoughts of self-harm and suicide.

As I grew up, the pain did too. When I was fourteen, my mom had my little brother Liam. Her pregnancy with him was a difficult one due to her having placenta previa which is where the placenta covers the opening of the cervix. She began to bleed and had to be brought to a hospital in Sioux Falls, SD, for monitoring. She was there for a long time. Liam was born by C-section and was premature by three months. He stayed in the hospital for a long time.

I went to visit my mom and him in the NICU. I was holding him, and as my mom went to get the camera to take a picture, he went bradycardic. Which is where his heart rate would slow down to lower than 60 beats per min. The alarms started to sound, and nurses rushed over. After that I never went back to see him because I was scared of him dying in my arms if it were to happen again.

Liam finally came home, but he was on a monitor to make sure he was breathing. It was always scary when it would go off in the middle of the night, and my mother would rush to him. As he got older, there wasn't a need for the monitor. He is a spunky guy and full of life. It was hard to have a good relationship with him because I was so much older than he was and soon got my first job. I love both my little brothers dearly and wish I had more time for them.

I became a teenager, and the relationship between my mother and I started to deteriorate. One morning we got into a fight about shoes. She wanted to wear the shoes my dad got me but all the clothes that he bought me I would never wear because they were special to me.

My mom called me a bitch which led me to my next actions. We had an early out from school, so I took the opportunity to pack all my stuff up. I was ready to leave and live with my dad. I called him and told him I needed a get-away car, but he said my mom would call him. I knew better.

When my mom got home, I asked quietly if I could go live with my dad. She responded in anger and opened my door and saw all my stuff packed up.

Darren was helping my mom who was crying. I was trying to get a hold of my dad to come get me, but my phone was dying. It got to the point where I just left the house and started walking in the snow toward the highway to walk to my dad's. Darren caught up to me in his truck and brought me back home. They were both crying and telling me that they loved me.

I went to my dad's that night but later on my mom came for me and I went back with her. I couldn't leave my younger brothers the way my older brothers had left me. It hurt me to think of my little brothers being alone, so I stayed.

Although we had our problems, my mom threw me a 'Twilight' themed birthday party. She got me the movie and made cupcakes with cherry filling and decorated them with vampire teeth. It was one of the better times at home. She went out of her way to help me and support me, but I was too angry and depressed to realize it.

By the eighth grade, I was tired of the torment. I went to the kitchen where my mom kept her medicine and I took five pills out of a bottle from top of the microwave and swallowed them down with whiskey. Sadly, I woke up the next day.

When I was thirteen, my dad remarried to my now stepmom, Claire. She was so warm and kind. My dad's house on fifth avenue changed quite drastically after she moved in. The laundry was no longer on the table but in baskets. She also left me a note one day telling me that there were feminine products behind the toilet paper so if I ever needed them, they were there.

Moving forward to ninth grade. I was still in depression trying to deal with the abuse and faults in my own life. Anger got the best of me as I grew older because I wasn't taught how to regulate emotions. I became hostile and would hurt my classmates.

One day I was sitting with a friend when a girl approached me and began to talk 'crap' about me. I confronted her, and she pushed me into a wall where I retaliated by punching her in the face breaking her glasses. She then ran and told the teacher and I got in school suspension.

While in middle school not only did the kids bully me but my gym teacher did as well. He thought it was funny how quick to anger I was. He would step on the backs of my shoes and tease me, so I threatened to take a baseball bat and crack his skull. He laughed and said he'd like to see me try and that he could "drop kick" me before I had the chance.

My anger usually got the best of me. I wouldn't think about consequences I would just react, hence the classmates calling me "psycho". When I turned fifteen, I met a girl named Britt. I befriended her and soon found out she was pregnant.

I stood up for her when people would be mean to her about the pregnancy. At one point, I shoved a boy into the wall because Britt had been laying on the ground and he ran up saying, "Spontaneous abortion!" and was going to kick her.

We were both on the cheer-leading squad when I met her brother, Cole, not long after, I started to date Cole. This would be the biggest mistake I had made. I was trapped with him for about eight months.

The first month together was OK, but then he became angry and didn't care about how he treated me. He began pushing me into walls and spitting on me. He even would throw things on the floor and say, "Bitch, pick it up!" I was worried what would happen to me if I didn't do what he said. I remember crying at work because he and his family were so volatile.

While working at McDonald's, I met Mitchel, my now husband. We closed the store together a lot after I turned sixteen and could work late. We started to work together more, and I asked him if he played Xbox. He said he did, and I got his gamer-tag which then led to him asking me for my phone number, and we talked until about 4 am.

Meeting Mitchel was life-changing. I was still with Cole, but I was over him and was trapped. Mitchel brought a new light and life to me.

One day I went to McDonald's crying because I had to go to break up with Cole. It was a mutual break up, but Cole and his family were crazy. When I arrived at their house, they locked all the doors and stood in front of them until they were ready for me to leave.

After the breakup, I finally felt free. I was finally rid of the family. I got a restraining order on Cole because he would come into McDonald's and make messes like smearing ketchup all over the tables knowing I had to clean them. He also poured pop on my vehicle.

When I started to hang out with Mitchel, Cole saw us together in a car. It was our first time hanging out and Cole wouldn't stop calling and texting me. Mitchel wasn't sure about hanging out with me, but he stayed, and we went to Mt. Lake for a walk and to hang out at a park. I remember Cole calling me telling me I can't hang out with other boys. In the background, his sisters were yelling for him to leave me alone.

As time passed and Mitchel and I began to date, Cole threatened to get some friends and jump him or beat him up. That night I followed Cole to McDonald's and told him if he wanted to fight that I would fight him. He stated, "We already know from our relationship that I can beat you." He proceeded to call me a whore and slut. The cops were coming so I went to my car and left.

Mitchel and I parked by the cemetery where I broke down crying. Mitchel stayed with me until midnight that night and came over the next morning to make sure I was OK. At this time, I never met someone who cared so much about my well-being.

When I was sixteen, my dad wanted to throw me an extravagant birthday party, but I declined because I didn't have any friends at that point.

This brings me to my first day of Junior year. I had a verbal altercation with my principal. I had closed at work the night before and I was not in the mood to deal with people. He approached me and tried talking to me, but I just brushed him off. He pulled me aside and told me I needed to show him respect. I told him that he had to earn my respect. From that time on, he had it out for me.

Soon after Mitchel and I started to date, he went to college where I only saw him on the weekends. He was always there for me coming down when I needed him the most.

One day my mom and I got into a fight over my phone. I left and went to the park knowing that things were going to go south. When I came back home, I asked to go to my dad's for the night. My mom took my keys and threw them at me and pushed me into the wall. I ran outside and asked my stepdad if I could go to my dad's, he said, "Sure."

My mom came out yelling at me and I pushed her into the grill and took off running where she then caught up to me and pulled me down and sat on top of me and pinned me down. I was yelling, telling her to get off of me. I didn't realize that my little brother who was just five years old was watching this altercation.

Although my mom and I had our verbal and physical fights, she is still my mom and I do love her. We have a better relationship now than when I was younger. I think it's because she was in denial about things being wrong with me.

At sixteen, I started to take anti-depressants. First Celexa and then changed to Lexapro. I talked to my doctor about the possibility of me being bipolar, but she said I would have to see a psychiatrist, which never happened.

At this point in time, I was a manager at McDonald's, but I was tired of the politics and bad blood that was there since the employees were split between being on my side vs. Cole's mom's side, who also worked there. I brought in my uniform and quit and didn't show up for any other shifts.

I then got a job at Hy-Vee as a courtesy clerk/checker and soon moved up to kitchen clerk which paid more. It was the summer of 2013 when I got a second job at the nursing home in our town. I was a CNA and since they paid for my certification, I worked there until it was time for college.

I originally was going to go to school for elementary education to teach kindergarten, but I changed to nursing after I did my clinical at a nursing home. There I saw a woman who was bleeding from a sore on her bottom. I told the nurses and they stated that they knew and said that it happens all the time. I saw the type of care that the elderly people had, and it made me sick, so I wanted to be a nurse who would take good care of the residents.

Chapter Two
On My Own

I began school in fall of 2013 at Minnesota State, Mankato, for pre-nursing. I moved in with Mitchel. I also had accepted a position at an assisted/independent living facility which was three stories.

After a while, I had more rages of anger, suicidal thoughts and still depression. I was finally able to get a referral to a counselor, Barbara. I met with Barbara, and she was a nice petite woman who had a welcoming smile that put me at ease. During this time, we did a diagnostic assessment, which led to the diagnosis of bipolar disorder, anxiety, and borderline personality disorder in October of 2013.

I still remember when I told Mitchel, he said, "No matter what you're diagnosed with, you're the still the same person you woke up as today." That night he took me out for dinner and a movie to try and cheer me up. I had just started school and went to Student Health Services to meet with a nurse practitioner to start medications. I met with Dr. E and she received my records and first put me on the anti-psychotic Latuda. It was hard learning when to time my medications right. I was still unstable.

Mitchel was walking on eggshells around me because I was so unpredictable with my mood swings. I was tired all the time and stopped showing up for work and was calling in all the time. I remember being so depressed and suicidal that I laid in bed with a knife while Mitchel was at work, contemplating taking my life. I never did anything because I realized that there is much more to live for.

I had therapy each week with Barbara as medications were getting figured out. I did well on Latuda, but it was too expensive and wasn't covered by insurance, so I had to look at what was available to me. Dr. E then changed my medications to Geodon, Vistaril, and still Citalopram. I remember not being fond of this medication as I felt sick from all I was taking.

The mental state I was in was unstable and unpredictable not only for myself but for Mitchel as well. I took all my anger and frustration on him and looking back I hate myself for how I treated him. After the diagnosis in October of 2013 the fall passed, and I was going into the ER almost every weekend. It was one-hundred-dollar copay per visit, but I had no choice.

In the spring of 2014, I had been on medication for a while but still wasn't sure about timing it because it made me drowsy. My job as a CNA was short lived at the assisted living as one night, I wanted to die so I was going to jump from the third story. Luckily a nurse could come in and take my shift and that night I went to the ER.

At the ER I was put in a room with no windows and that just had a mat on the floor to lay on. Mitchel was there with me. I was angry and pacing around the room; they weren't giving me my medication and were trying to find placement. I had asked for a snack and they gave me a Pepsi and some animal crackers. The caffeine didn't help as it just helped fuel me.

The nurse came in and I had bad repetitive thoughts and was yelling, and security came in. I just hugged and tucked myself into Mitchel for safety. At about 3 a.m. I was wheeled up to the fourth floor where the behavioral health unit was. Mitchel stood outside the locked doors watching me go into the unit knowing he couldn't come with me.

I wasn't sure about the unit and stayed in my room since I was tired. I slept a lot but when Mitchel would come visit, I would do my best to look good by taking a shower and changing clothes. One day he brought me flowers to put in my room. He also brought his sweater in, so I could wear it since it was cold, and it was comforting.

While at the hospital they put me back on Latuda and gave me sample packs and coupons to try and afford it. I was doing well and was there for five days. After the hospitalization I talked to Barbara about my job and she said she didn't think it was a healthy workplace for me.

I quit my job over text and never went back, just to visit. I made the mistake of going back there and visiting my favorite resident. She asked me why I wasn't working, and I just told her the truth about my mental illness. I then received a letter from the company that I was no longer allowed on their property.

After my hospitalization I needed to find a new job and since I still had my CNA certification, I found a position at another nursing home doing overnights. I also was referred to a new psychiatrist, Deb. I was only with Deb shortly before she moved to the county and not at the clinic. I then changed doctors to Dr. Mag. I was still taking the Latuda, so I told my coworkers that I may get tired. It wasn't the best job for me because I was taking seventeen credits at school and had finals on the days I was scheduled to work. I worked at this job for about a month, but my body couldn't take it anymore, so I put my two weeks in, but never finished them out.

Money was tight while Mitchel worked at Target and I had no job. I applied to work at Hy-Vee as a kitchen clerk. They never called me about an interview, so I called and talked to HR to see if they still had the opening. They liked me over the phone, so I got the interview secured and after that they hired me. It was a decent job. It didn't pay well but I did get the hours I needed, and they accommodated my school schedule.

I was meeting with Dr. Mag once a month as the insurance was only covering twelve appointments for a year. The insurance company wasn't covering any of the bill, it was about $550.00 per visit. She would change my medications to put me on Seroquel and Lamictal.

As the year of 2014 continued, Mitchel proposed to me. We were at a park in Alexandria, MN, and there was a pond iced over and people were skating. There was a lone bench there and Mitchel wanted us to sit on it. I was apprehensive, but we did. Then two boys come over and pushed us around the ice. Mitchel was telling me how much he loved me and talked about our relationship. I ruined the proposal by asking, "Why don't you propose already?!"

He stated, "Well, your dad said no," then he pulled out the ring. I was in shock and so happy, but I felt bad because I tried to joke with him, but it just came off rude. Little did I know that his sister, Nadalie, was hiding in a snowbank taking pictures of us throughout the proposal. I was ecstatic because my dad gave him the permission after he attempted to talk to him one time before where he said no.

After the good times came the bad. My dad who had cancer became sicker and was hospitalized at Windom Area Hospital. It was late October to early November when things started to deteriorate quickly. Mitchel and I were going

24

to get married at the hospital, so my dad could be a part of it, but we decided not to and to spend time with my dad instead.

November 6th 2014 was the day my father passed away. The day he passed all the family was around him, and as he took his last breath, he smiled at me. Knowing that he was going to heaven made it much easier on us.

I went back to work after my dad's memorial. My co-workers at Hy-Vee gave me a sympathy card, but I was soon to leave that job to go into an assisted living again. I began work at another nursing home in 2014. I worked there so I could keep my CNA certification. I enjoyed my co-workers and the residents. It was busy, and I was changing medications again. I tried Paliperidone in the spring of 2015 while still taking Seroquel and Lamictal. I would bring my meds with me in the morning, so I wouldn't forget them, but one day I left them in an unlocked locker. When a coworker found the medication, she brought it to the nurse. They then put in the weekly update about not having medications around.

Chapter Three
The First Stages of Schizophrenia

In 2015 I began the fight against psychosis. I was working at a local nursing home when the symptoms began. When they first began, it was a whisper of about two to three different voices. They were inaudible, like a murmur. It was almost too quiet to understand. At the nursing home we had walkie talkies and I had it hanging on my hip. When I heard the voices, I thought it was the walkie talkie. So, I turned it off and listened and the voices were still there. I was confused so I turned it back on and went outside the resident's room while doing their laundry. No one was there. It was empty. I just disregarded the voices and didn't think much of it at the time.

After the auditory hallucinations, the visual hallucinations began as well. These were more frightening than the voices I first heard. The worst hallucinations that still haunt me were the first nights with the black figures. The black figures were demonic figures. They were people-shaped shadowy figures.

The first night that I saw the one figure I could feel someone watching me and as I awoke to that feeling, I saw a figure pacing around the end of my bed trying to get to me. I screamed and grabbed my phone for the light. I screamed, "BABE!" I was in fear for my life. Mitchel came in and calmed me down reassuring me nothing was there. He let me sleep with the door open that night.

The next night I could feel the eyes looking at me and the pressure on the bed. I woke up and there the figure was again, but this time sitting on my bed and watching me sleep. I wasn't sure what to do so I covered my head and prayed it would go away.

The third consecutive night was one that still terrifies me to this day. Once again, I felt the presence and I awoke, and he was there standing over me. He was watching and waiting to see what I would do. As I recognized who it was, he burst into flames in my room. I assume he went back to hell since I felt like this is where he came from. This was something of a phenomenon. I usually get asked if I was in a daze or was still tired at the time, but I was not. I was in more of a fight-or-flight state due to the severity of the hallucination.

The best part of 2015 was getting married to my wonderful husband, Mitchel.

In 2016 I applied for my dream job at Mayo Clinic Health System on their Behavioral Health Unit. I had the interview and it went well and I started orientation on the 23rd of February 2016. I was happy to leave working with the elderly and move on to where I wanted to be a nurse.

During the summer of 2016 I had my first hospitalization at New Ulm. After being hospitalized there, they changed my medications from Paliperidone to Risperidone. While at the hospital, I fainted from the medication change, but it was OK. The nurses helped me and gave me a bell to ring if I needed to get up. While there I had Dr. M who said that what I was experiencing was just anxiety and nothing more.

I missed work due to the hospitalization and was talked to about it and asked if it would happen again. I stated that if it flares up again, I might need to have more time off. I was still experiencing psychosis after the hospitalization and went to see Barbara for after care.

The following entries are from my personal journal which depict my life in the beginning of the fight with schizophrenia. It also includes progress notes from stays at facilities.

The journals are *italic,* and the progress notes are in **bold.**

July 5th 2016 – After First Hospitalization at New Ulm

Today is a good day. I lay in bed until 11 am. I wasn't sleeping, just dreaming about different things. I decided to get most of my goals done. So far, I dropped off my documentation for nursing school and bought a new journal for myself. My goal is to write in it every day and read the previous day or the journals for the week to see if there is a pattern but with the Risperidone it has gotten better.

Today I haven't had any paranoia except for the bug that is in our apartment. I was able to walk around the mall without feeling like someone was going to kill me. It was weird to think that I had been that sick and wasn't able or didn't want to get help. I know now that next time if it gets bad again, I will go in and get help. I am glad that Mitchel took me in. If it wasn't for him, I wouldn't have gone in.

I know and feel like my stay at the hospital was bad and good at the same time. It was bad because I missed home but was so sick that I couldn't function. I do think that I may have been annoying because of how sick I was to the nurses. The staff was nice. I'm glad it was very strict and structured because it was just what I needed. I'm working toward creating that same structure at home and work. I'm still worried about going back to work since I'm not trying to take the extra PRN (as needed medication) unless needed.

I was happy I was able to wean myself off the PRN Seroquel in the morning and can function without it. I am happy that I am out of the hospital, and I'm still trying to fulfill my goals. I'm healthy, happy, and future orientated.

After being at New Ulm it was time for me to get ready for school while working 40 hours every two weeks at Mayo Clinic. Spring of 2016 I was a tutor for biochemistry and anatomy and physiology 1. I attended a school event for pre-nursing students at South Central College where I handed in my application. I was accepted after taking my entrance exam and having a 3.25GPA. I began in fall of 2016. The place I tutored they wanted me to continue to tutor, but I declined due to being in the nursing program and wouldn't have free time.

July 6th 2016

7:40 pm, I took my PRN med (Seroquel 50mg) for paranoia. I am home now and its evening. I was doing well this morning when I wrote, but now, I am having paranoia. I'm telling myself I am safe, but the different noises are making me anxious and worried. It hasn't gotten to the point of being scared for my life, but I am hyper-vigilant about noises, voices, and other things. I'm hoping it will go away.

July 7ᵗʰ 2016 – PRN Taken at 6:53 pm

I did well today. I got a little worried about people and noises. Tonight, the upstairs neighbors came by and I was letting Jazmine out and our neighbor was in his car on the phone. I immediately fear that they are plotting to kill me. I locked the doors, shut the shades and turned off all the lights. Mitchel is still at work. I'm hoping that we will still go to his parents and see 'Finding Dory'. I think I'll be OK. I just have to tell myself I am safe. Upping Risperidone to 1 mg at bedtime. While on the way to Mitchel's parents I was paranoid – people are out to get me, and I couldn't look into anything that showed reflections because I saw something in the glass of the cabinet. This lasted for about four hours.

July 8ᵗʰ 2016

Was at Mitchel's parents' house everything went great. We got home, and we watched Jim Jeffries and I got very happy and had trouble sleeping.

July 9ᵗʰ 2016

I had a good morning, but Mitchel was late for work and I had to bring him food. We are both stressed about his job at the gym. I started having trouble at 4:30 when we went to the gym. We were there for an hour. I did well but there was a guy wearing a hoodie. I got nervous around him. I kept on an eye on him while I was working out. I went up to Mitchel and the guy went behind me to a machine and I got paranoid and started walking back and forth and making my scared noise.

We got home, and all was well until I heard noises from the laundry room and got worried there were people here to try and get inside the house and hurt us. Mitchel made me take my PRN (as needed) med at 6:30 pm. I didn't want to take it, but he told me I'm still sick. It makes me worried again for the evening shift I have to work this Monday. I'm going to take my meds at 8:00 pm while at work and hope that helps.

My main concern is working with mentally ill patients and whether or not I'll feed off of it. I'm rethinking my job on the behavioral health unit. I'll have to see how it goes on Monday.

July 10th 2016

Today was a good day except I felt weird this morning. I can't even name the feeling just weird. Not upset but oddly content with no desire to do anything. Mitchel suggested a PRN at 2:00–2:30 pm. We are trying to level out meds and mood still. Tomorrow will be the true test with work tonight. I'm going to take my meds at 8:00–8:30 pm and stay up late and wake up early tomorrow and clean the house or at least do the dishes. I'll try to be up by 9:00am and clean, have coffee, and shower for work.

July 11th 2016

Work went well. Meds taken at 8:00–8:30 pm at work. I didn't fall asleep and no mood dis-regulation.

July 12th 2016

I had my nursing school meeting and it was stressful because the books are over two grand, but Mitchel said he's going to help decide what books I should reserve.

July 13th 2016

Today I did a 13-hour shift and it went well, no PRN's. Meds taken at 9:00 pm. I felt frisky and wanted to play. I felt like a giggling child that wanted to play with my beanie babies or stuffed animals. I also had the feeling that something was in my hands. I had this feeling on my hands like there was something on them and that something should be there. I kept feeling like something or someone was in Mitchel, like I would look away and I felt his eyes rolled over and would look at me, but he said he wasn't looking at me. It scares me because I feel like it's something else although a part of me knows it's him. It's always difficult to realize when it is real or not.

July 21st 2016

I've had trouble lately. I saw the shadow of the thing the other night even though Mitchel was there. I had angry outbursts the other day when Mitchel came home and got mad at myself about not doing anything with the house or at all. He came home and was angry and was complaining about me.

I said, "Fuck It!" and got up throwing clothes around. He was getting ready to shower when I came in with the laundry basket and put clothes in it. I wouldn't speak except for, "I'm fine." He then yelled at me, "What do you want from me!? I'm working 50-60 hours a week." I said, "Nothing, I don't need anything." I began throwing clothes in the wash.

When I came back, I was still angry. I was in the bedroom taking clothes off the desk and throwing them on the bed. I got angrier as I stewed about it. Then the fan was in the way, so I picked it up and threw it on the ground with force. It didn't break though. After the clothes were on the bed I was still raging and threw the brown laundry basket against the wall.

Mitchel comes in and says, "What are you doing?" he then tries to be nice and starts folding laundry. I told him that I didn't need his help, but he insisted. After that I was in the kitchen while he ate and got angry again. I picked up the Tupperware that was in my way and threw it at the wall. I just had so much rage that I couldn't do anything to get it out.

That brings me to tonight I got home from work and was watching Grey's Anatomy. Suddenly, I started to feel weird and angry and how I used to feel. I was just waiting for Mitchel to make one mistake or do something wrong, so I could blow up and release all the rage. I am not able to use coping skills when this happens. I don't realize the damage I do until after I have done it. The rage fits cause me to 'black out' and not realize how mean or destructive I am.

Mitchel and I had a long talk about how it makes him feel when I rage out and he expressed that it scares him and is worried that I would hurt him. We got on the subject that if I were to hurt him or throw something at him, he would call the cops and press charges on me.

It makes me upset because I can't control the anger or realize in the moment what's happening. The thought made me upset that he would do this to his wife. It was a long conversation and my moods were switching in seconds again. They upped my Seroquel to 100mg three times a day plus what I take at nighttime. I'm confused about why they didn't do anything with the Risperidone but maybe it's because my doctor is going on maternity leave.

July 25ᵗʰ 2016

We went to Valley Fair yesterday. We spent most of the time in the waterpark. We went on a water slide with one of Mitchel's coworkers but while waiting in line I started to get paranoid. I saw a person who made me uncomfortable then my mind wandered into thinking that someone had done something to the slide, and we were going to go over the edge and die.

It was a far stretch – is what Mitchel said to me – but that's what my head does while I am paranoid. I still realize that there is something I do physically to try and cope and I make a 'hum' noise and will pace or pace in place. I'm still taking the 100mg three times a day but I'm not seeing much effect except for being tired. Tonight, Mitchel had me go to the gym with him. I was OK until we got there but I started to get paranoid about Mitchel's coworkers and felt like other people were looking at me. I was able to distract myself long enough for him to finish, but still got paranoid while we were leaving. Once we were home, I was OK.

July 26ᵗʰ 2016

I'm not sure if the date is correct but the other night, I had auditory hallucinations. I had someone breathing in my ear and I could feel it. I was able to get up because Mitchel didn't hear me calling for him. I was scared, so he came in and we talked but I was too drugged up and tried to figure things out.

July 28ᵗʰ 2016

Today I had my therapy appointment with Barbara. We did talk about the delusional disorder and I also talked about how the paranoia and hallucinations haven't gone away. She told me to see about getting an appointment with another doctor while mine is on maternity leave. I contacted my doctor the next day and talked to a nurse about seeing the figure in my room again and paranoia. The doctor told me to increase the Risperidone to 1mg at night and 1mg in the morning while still taking the Seroquel too. I work Friday, Saturday, Sunday but have a doctor appointment Tuesday at 8:30am.

July 30th 2016

I was at work until 11:30 pm and I'm not able to take my meds at work because the 300mg of Seroquel will drug me out. Since I can't take the medication at work, I became paranoid that something is following me at work.

There was also a problem at home with the random guy doing laundry. There was something off about him in our laundry room. He had no soap, no basket, and all his clothes lying about the room. This started making me paranoid about how he got in and what he knew about us. I was unsure if he was after me. He must have been looking/watching the house to see where it's vulnerable.

I also had a bout of paranoia at work. While the nurses on the unit were discussing past clients that had been sick and experienced hallucinations and delusions. I started to feel alert and scared that the thing is around me. It's gotten to the point where it happens at work, but the Risperidone was increased and plus it has made me dizzy to the point where I couldn't shower and was worried about making it to work.

August 1st 2016

I was doing OK except for napping all day. We had McDonald's for supper. After supper we showered. We watched one episode of 'Game of Thrones'. After the show, I started to get paranoid about noises although it was just our landlord, Joel. I started thinking about the random guy but then we started watching 'Breaking Bad'. I had a bad thought about hurting someone on TV, because my mind was telling me they were real, and I could touch them. I'm still confused as to why this happened. I'm also worried about Mitchel's job at Planet Fitness. I'm worried that it's going to cause me anxiety and delusions because I'm the jealous type. He said I need to learn to get over it.

August 7ᵗʰ 2016

I've been doing well this week. I haven't heard or seen anything. My mood has been off, but especially at work. My patience has gotten low for the patients I work with. The first code green I had was scary.

Bringing me to tonight – Sunday – we went to see Suicide Squad. It was a good movie, but I have trouble with big crowds, and it was a full house. I became aware of a few people especially the man next to me. I thought he was looking at me all the time, but I guess he wasn't. The problem I have is that while we were in the movie my mind was battling itself about whether or not to kill or hurt people. My mind kept playing scenarios in my mind I felt like a crazy person.

At the end I prepared myself to defend myself from the suspicious people. I felt like there was going to be a fight. It isn't until Mitchel puts me in check does my mind stop the thinking for the moment. Once that moment is over though, my mind goes back to thinking and creating images and videos of what I could be doing. It was images of me yelling at people. One was slitting a man's throat and I just don't know why it happens. I was telling myself stop and to not think about it.

It was a battle, like a wall breaks again. And I have paranoia/anger come out and I can't build the wall up before it gets knocked down again. Mitchel says I need to figure something out because this always happens in a large crowd of people; I really thought someone was going to come after us or shoot up the theater. I just feel a little psychotic where my mind continues to go around and around with thoughts.

August 11ᵗʰ 2016

I have been doing OK except yesterday I was worried about Mitchel's coworkers and another person that Mitchel talked to. I was worried that Mitchel was going to get hurt or something bad was going to happen. I was able to make it through the gym time which was an hour.

August 15th 2016

Today is Monday and I have the day off from working the weekend. I had trouble at work with a manic patient because my patience was limited due to them behaving uncontrollable. I did apologize but I'm not sure if she heard it. One of the patients is leaving today he's been here for like two months so it's sad to see him go but is also a good thing. We had a new patient who has lice and was very belligerent. All she wanted was her clothes, but she couldn't have them because they were contaminated with lice.

It was a tough night, but we made it through, which brings me to this morning. Mitchel and I finally had some time together between our schedules, so we had breakfast and coffee together and watched 'Good Mythical Morning'. It's pretty funny with some of their challenges they do.

I took Jazmine to the vet to get her nails trimmed. I could tell the vet tech wasn't happy with the condition of her nails. They want us to take her on walks to keep her nails shorter. Her nail quick was long so they have to wait for it to recede. After the vet I went to hand in my CPR certification to one of the members of the nursing program, so all my documentation is complete, and I am ready for school to start.

It does kind of make me nervous I was ready to start reading or start assignments, but I don't know what they are. I am hoping that my meds won't affect my studies.

I hope I'll be organized enough to complete assignments and go to class on little sleep. I'm sure I'll be able to manage, and I should also be getting my computer back soon.

Pretty soon I'll be completely ready for school. My scrubs for school haven't come, they but say its delayed. On the bright side my mood has been stable except that I get tired easily because I take 100mg of Seroquel three times a day. Work has been good. The nurses seem to like me.

August 17th 2016

Last night I heard the voices again but this time there were three different ones. Two male and one female whispering to each other about me. Mitchel was in the bathroom while this was happening.

Today I visited my little brothers. It went OK except they had friends over, so I ended up having to talk to my mom. It didn't go very well. I'm tired of trying to have a relationship. It just makes me sad that my mom still doesn't want a relationship or if she does, she doesn't know how to.

After the sadness went away Mitchel and I snuggled but by that time the meds kicked in, so I was now drugged up. Mitchel finds it funny because I usually don't remember what happens after it. Although we were having a good time when he tucked me into bed his face changed in the dark appearing like he was being used as a host.

It was dark, the eyes were angry, and the face was pulling away like it was stuck in one part but moving in the other. When I saw it again, it was a face with teeth bared and eyes that were dark. I was so scared, and I thought the things had control of Mitchel.

He doesn't understand that it is inside of him. It's gotten stronger. First it appears to me in the bedroom at night, later at work, at school, then the hospital. The next step for them was appearing when Mitchel was in bed with me.

I'm trying to figure out if I need something else to protect myself or if this is it. What has been given to me. As the days go by it only gets worse and more complex. I think they are slowly coming to get me, and the figures are appearing clearer now.

Barbara and I went through the DSM-5 to try and narrow down the diagnosis. As of then she had me ad Bipolar – 1 with Psychotic Features. We contemplated schizophrenia, schizoaffective, and delusional disorder. I was still young, about nineteen when the battle of psychosis took hold, so she was unsure about the diagnosis of Schizophrenia. I was experiencing what are known as positive symptoms like hallucinations and delusions while I wasn't displaying much of the negative symptoms.

September 2nd 2016

It's the second week of school and the nursing program is a hot mess. My classes are very disorganized, and I feel like I'm a little behind, but I know I can get caught up.

October 15th 2016

It's been a bit heavy lately. After therapy the other day I realized that there were things wrong with our relationship. Mainly that I am a burden; I talked to Mitchel about it, but he didn't say much. I've been really bad lately with taking my medication, I've either been out of it or completely forget about it. I had clinical at a nursing home where I had my own resident and I had to do a physical exam on them for the grade. I passed with a 60/66 since I forgot one body system. I was also really tired from my medication. I didn't pass pharmacology fall of 2016 so I had to re-sequence and take it spring of 2017.

December 29th 2016

It's been quite a change since I last wrote. We have moved into a house and I have to retake a course next semester. I had to come clean about my mental health in an appeal to retake a course. At this point they still have me diagnosed with Bipolar 1 – with psychotic features and Borderline Personality Disorder.

Working and school was becoming too hard. During this time, I was still unstable with my medications. I was taking Seroquel and Lamictal and Risperidone. I was having trouble with auditory hallucinations at school, home, and work. I would hear them call my name when I would be in class which was very distracting not knowing who or what was talking to me.

I thought it was the demons that caused my paranoia. At this point I decided to step out of the nursing program because my mental illness was affecting my work. Since the Risperidone wasn't working, we tried Vraylar, a new medication. I then pursued just an associate degree the spring of 2017.

Chapter Four
Finding the Way to Truth

March 5th 2017

Today we are visiting Mitchel's parents' house for a birthday supper. I just changed medications from Risperidone to Vraylar. We aren't sure if it will be covered by insurance, but my doctor gave me coupons for it. The cost of the medication was high. It was $50.00 per bottle and I was increasing the dose fast. I was able to get a month supply free.

My doctor said that I would get worse before I got better. So far, I'm still aware of people and am scared of cops. I'm thinking that I will be pulled over and it will be a fake cop. I am worried that they will try to hurt or rape me. These thoughts happen every night driving home from work. Projections of visions of the figure walking and coming into the house and standing in the doorway watching me.

I was doing OK to begin with today but as the night came, I started to see people in my in-law's house. I told Mitchel and he had me move away from the windows to the couch. I remember thinking repetitive thoughts that people were out there. I could feel my in-laws watching me, they have been really good about trying to help me get better.

March 6th 2017

Today is my birthday and we are going to celebrate. With the med change we can't leave Mankato, but we went shopping and watched the movie Logan. While in the theater people began to cough and my mind told me that there was poisonous gas in the air or that someone released anthrax in the theater.

March 7th 2017

I had my first day back to work during my med change. I was working in the ICU for the night. It kept me busy, but I felt off. I was worried about walking to my vehicle as I parked far away by the bushes. I thought someone was waiting for me. I called Mitchel while I walked to my car. No one is there though. When I got home, I took my meds but kept getting startled and worried when the furnace goes off. It makes a growling sound. I also hear footsteps in the house following me. Mitchel and I came up with a code word to help tell me when my thoughts are 'crazy'. The code word was 'Aliens'. On my way home from work, I was listening to Christian music and felt like God was inside me and we were connected.

March 10th 2017

Today was a good day so far except that my mind keeps wandering into theories.

This is how I think/feel today. It began two years ago when the dark figures came. The figure appeared in my bedroom at our apartment.

The first night I saw it pace around my bed. The next night it was sitting on my bed I could feel the weight on the bed and my leg. The third night it was standing next to my bed staring at me and then burst into flames. It went away for a while but came back.

During this time, I started to hear multiple voices whispering at me. I couldn't make out what they were saying to me. I would hear them at school/home/ work. It got worse to when they would call my name. Later, the figure came back and appeared in my bedroom.

It was there for multiple days and lasted months. It was always the same thing standing in my bedroom at the end of the bed and next to me.

The voices and visions got worse, but I was also paranoid. I was worried about people coming into my house. I could always feel/hear people outside the apartment. One night I locked myself in my bedroom with no lights on. I was underneath a blanket so if someone looked through the window no one would see or hear me. This led me to go to the hospital where the figure followed me.

I feel that this thing has been with my family for years. It began with my dad when he was younger, he had a voice come and tell him to kill himself. I believe that the figure I see had followed my dad through his life.

I remember when I was about nine, I saw the figure at the farmhouse. I was lying in bed with worship music playing and my glitter lamp on. Standing in my doorway was the black figure leaning up against the door frame. I believe that this figure was watching me for a reason. I think it followed my dad through his life and when he passed away this figure moved onto me. That's why everywhere I go, I can see it or feel its presence around me. Mitchel doesn't believe this, but I know this is true.

I'll speed up to now, we live in a different place. I still get paranoid at our new house because of all the noises. I think someone will try to break in and rape me, so, I don't turn the lights on at night. The problem here at the house is that the figure has still appeared and shown itself to me in the backyard. I was letting the dogs out and there it was by the tree and it began walking toward me at a brisk paced. I got my dog inside the house and was able to lock the door before it came in.

Now it is March and I changed medications since the voices and visions of the figure haven't stopped. I feel like the new meds are working. Since I don't hear the voices or the figure except in my mind where it shows me in flashbacks of what happened. It's like a whole year's worth of visions being played in my mind. Then seeing it in the bedroom and when it took over Mitchel's face and showed me its true form.

I feel like this figure is evil and wants to hurt me. On my way home, this past week I came to the realization that God has put himself inside of me using me as a vessel who will protect me from the dark figures. It feels like God put a force-field around our house and that's why the figures can only stay in the backyard.

It gets harder at night when I let the dogs out my mind projects the past and it scares me. I have to look down and repeat phrases to try and keep calm. I believe that all of this is connected somehow to my father and his passing.

March 15th 2017

3:15pm went to Planet Fitness to see if Mitchel needed food. He didn't. I went to Barnes and Noble to see about books on bipolar disorder. I found one and bought it. I got coffee at the coffee shop there. As I sat there, I saw a table of four talking; they would look at me and then go back to talking. My head started to hurt, and I believe they were trying to read my thoughts. I felt uncomfortable and left.

I was headed to the bipolar support group. As the people started to come in, I had overwhelming anxiety as they looked at me. My head began to hurt; I could feel their mind's power as they tried to get my information through my thoughts.

I was waiting for the being to take over me and put a conforming force-field around me to stop them. I stayed for the whole group but could still feel them. This feeling lasted until 10:00 pm. If they retrieved my information they would 'clone' or create another Savanah but in a different body.

I got a new bottle of Lamotrigine from the pharmacy. There was a piece of paper glued to it. When I opened it, the safety seal came too easily. I was apprehensive about taking the medication as I thought it was laced with drugs. Mitchel made me take it despite my fears.

March 19th 2017

Yesterday in the morning, I was having coffee when I heard a woman's voice talking to me. I couldn't make out what they were saying. Then I went to hang out with Nadalie, so I wouldn't have to be alone. At night we were at home and I was sitting in the chair and I heard footsteps in the kitchen and clanging dishes but no one else was home. When Mitchel got home, the voices came again.

I just am not sure how anything could come in because of the force-field around the house. Unless the thing has transferred into me to get recognized by the force-field. Maybe this is why other people wanted my information, so they could clone into me to come and torment me in my house.

Tonight, we were on our way home as I looked out the window to the river, I saw a figure standing there. I felt its presence follow us to the car as if it was following us home. I haven't seen anything yet at our house but earlier today I realize the force-field may have been compromised.

Since seeing that reflection I had trouble feeling like something is there, but we were watching X-Men and Mitchel wanted to snuggle. I had a blanket over my head a little then I felt something evil come over me and my hands *were not mine and they were capable of something, but I chose not to try. I feel like something evil had possessed me. My body and mind are in a battle between God and the Devil.*

March 21st 2017

Last night I took my first dose of Haldol. I felt like the floor was squishy. Reality was too real, and the colors were fine. I could see myself moving in slow motion and so was everyone else. Today I am at my mother in-laws since I can't be alone on this medication for side effect reasons. Today I feel I have super hearing and can hear people's blood and heart beating. There is also a fuzzy sound in my ears. 3:04pm started to get a headache like a fuzzy radio searching for a signal. I am more aware of things tonight and my hands are not mine.

Med-time – Bedtime 7:30 pm. I looked out the window and saw three figures standing there. Dark shadows that knew I was in the house and followed me to this house. My in-laws are helping me. I can feel the good force-field around the house.

March 22nd 2017

This morning I woke up with projections in my mind of three figures standing in our yard. I tried talking myself out of it, but I want Mitchel to be protected. I went back to sleep but awoke because of visions in my mind of when I am out of the house the force-field is with me. It conforms to my body, so I am unsure of what will happen if the figures attack me.

I was supposed to graduate that semester, but I then was hospitalized again in March 2017 at the recommendation of Doctor Mag.

I brought in a doctor's note explaining that I can't attend class because I was going to be hospitalized. I also brought a note to my boss about having to go back to the hospital. With this hospitalization they put me on Haldol. I was still seeing Barbara for a while, but she then told me she was moving her practice to the cities, so I went without therapy until I got my case manager, Kim. She then referred me to a psychology clinic where I met my now therapist, Missy. Here we did a diagnostic assessment and I was diagnosed with Schizoaffective Bipolar Type instead of Bipolar 1 with psychotic features.

March 23rd 2017 – Second Hospitalization at New Ulm

Its 3:00 am on Thursday. Last night I couldn't sleep as the vision of myself and three shadow men were in my head, I realized that these shadow figures could have been other patients. Someone may be under attack by the figures who will then prove to me that they are here. They could use the patients as a vessel to get me, but I have the force-field around me.

I don't know what will happen if someone were to touch me. If only the figures will be harmed. 6:55am I am watching TV with another patient when it gets fuzzy. I saw the figure in the TV. I heard a knocking at the nurse's stations. I was worried about the nurses being OK or if someone is there to hurt them.

7:30am starting to get a headache again. It feels like searching for signals this morning. I was drawing pictures of my visions of what I see, and I found that I am protected by the force field. But the black figures could come in by being a new person and take human form.

The force-field around me is different because all my information is protected because they can't get through the force-field by touch.

Another patient wanted to play a game with me, but I think he wanted to trap me for information about myself. I am unsure about these people. He tried speaking to me and asked me about my marriage or if I have kids. I replied, "No." I think he understood I didn't want to talk. I've been reflecting on many things. My roommate understood what I talked about and says she can see what I see. It feels like a revelation. I am not "crazy". Someone else could see. I wish I could show Mitchel these things, but I haven't found a way yet. 1:00 pm headache again still searching for the signal.

March 29th 2017 – Home

I can't turn the outside light on for Mitchel. I am worried they will know I'm in the house and come and get me. I feel like the force-field is not as strong as before.

March 30th 2017

I was driving home and was worried the cops would pull me over and hurt or rape me. When I got home, I saw three black figures standing in the yard just like my vision at the hospital. I did my best to run to the door. I was safe.

March 31st 2017

I'm having trouble being alone in the house. I keep seeing or projecting the images in my mind of the black figures. I've seen them standing in the yard before and I can feel them outside planning their attack. I don't think it will be blocked due to the force-field being compromised.

I can't see the purple covering of the house. I don't feel safe alone and call people so I'm not alone, to let them know I am having trouble, just in case something happens.

April 1st 2017

Driving home from Claire's I saw the shadow man in the backseat of my car. I felt its presence in there. I felt like there was a being inside my vehicle which could turn me into traffic without control.

April 15th 2017

It's been one week since April 3rd when I had my doctor appointment. We increased and gave a PRN for an increase for 5mg extra of Haldol. I take it every day at 2pm. This helps me a lot I haven't had any delusions/ hallucinations. My hands tremor at times but are easily handled except when I'm trying to do something like eat or hand out drinks at snack time. My tongue has tremors but aren't too noticeable unless I stick out my tongue fully. I'm hoping with the next appointment I will have an AIMS (Abnormal Involuntary Movement Scale) test, or they can give me something for the tremors. I have been feeling restless again at night. Mitchel thought it was from me being up too late, but I think I need a higher dose of Cogentin.

To my doctor from my husband, Mitchel:

I think Savanah should switch meds. It seems that this medication doesn't stop any of her delusional thinking. Every day she suffers from coming up with theories that are very unrealistic, but she believes them. Her theories are based on some delusions her mind projects – hears things, sees images, unnatural thinking, footsteps and voices, figures and fake scenarios, people taking information.

Mitchel read a pamphlet at the doctor's office that explained schizophrenia but when it was brought up to my doctor, she denied that I had it.

July 5th 2017

I heard a woman's voice calling out names. I could hear the keypad being pushed with a person there trying to get in.

July 6th 2017

Today I worked only a few hours. I was having trouble before the start of the shift. I was thinking about the people I have touched in the past. They have the information – where I live and could figure out the new code on the door.

At work I found out I would be on the medical/surgical floor. I didn't like it, but I did it anyway. I was struggling with the thoughts of people trying to project their minds to mine. The TV had been pushing on different thoughts about animals dying and the people who killed them not getting the justice they deserved.

Why is it that we as people take life like we are God? Some people like to think they are all powerful and have control over all beings. I still see the black figures in my mind standing at the door trying to get the code. These numbers are only known to Mitchel and me. The only way that they would know is if they knew my thoughts and actions at the keypad.

That is why I feel a small headache and feel peoples' projections on me, but my mind is sharp and keeping the thoughts at bay. Before they break into my mind, the wall I built will do no good if they are using force. I am at home now.

July 30th 2017

Today while leaving Caribou Coffee I saw an invisible man jump in my car backseat. I could feel him watching me. It got worse at work. I came home and took my PRN Haldol. I'm not OK, the man appeared when I was driving to Mankato with Mitchel. This man showed me other invisible people that were hiding as humans and that he was their leader. Mitchel had us stop in Lake Crystal to switch positions.

While driving I was unable to switch lanes because of all of the invisible people in the roads. He said I could have hurt someone not being able to drive very well. The invisible man hasn't presented a certain tone to me just there watching. I'm not sure if he would have been left out of the force field.

Right now, there is only a keypad lock that keeps me safe from the outside. I don't know what this invisible man may bring, whether he's good or evil like the black figures that are demons.

August 13th 2017

Today is a day where I am beginning to feel like I know what is going on with the invisible man that came into my life. It was a few weeks ago when the man jumped in my car as I drove to work. This man had showed me many things like when I was driving to Mankato and he revealed that the other drivers were invisible people in the bodies of the drivers. They were in the middle of the roads, so I couldn't switch lanes. I feel like the invisible beings are here to help and protect me from the demons I see. Today he held the door for me at work. I heard him singing when he first appeared. They protect me. I believe that these may be angels sent to protect me from the demons.

At this time, I had my third hospitalization at New Ulm. I had to plan around my work schedule, so I wouldn't miss any more work. We discussed my diagnosis. It had been changed from Bipolar – 1 with Psychotic Features to Schizoaffective Bipolar type. While there they had contacted my therapist and questioned her about my behaviors and her thoughts. At the hospital they changed my medication to Zyprexa, Haldol, and Seroquel. After meeting with Missy for a longer amount of time, she was leaning toward the diagnosis of Schizophrenia.

Chapter Five
New Beginnings

After the hospitalization I looked for other employment in the system of Mayo Clinic but instead found a job that was more accommodating at the community hospital in my town. In October of 2017 I began my job as a ward clerk. I loved my job and the people I worked with, but my mental illness caught up with me and I became delusional having both auditory and visual hallucinations that consumed me. I was taking 300 Seroquel, 5mg Haldol, and 20 of Zyprexa trying to function.

To start off the year of 2018 I stayed at the crisis facility for a week. After that stay I returned to work and continued to have problems and my doctor wasn't helping and told me to go to the hospital again. Since I didn't graduate Spring of 2017, I decided to change my major to OTEC or Administrative Assistant to expand my knowledge for my then current job. While at the crisis facility, I emailed my teacher of both my online courses. She said she would accommodate my late work, but I was already too far behind, so I had to withdraw from school once again.

January 17th 2018

There are particles in the air slowly gathering waiting to take form in the darkness. Once it is dark the particles take a form of beings. Beings unknown to me, but I am safe in the light. I am safe in the dark when Mitchel is here. He is the protector. In the living room I am free the beings can't take shape. We need to form a barrier.

Admission: Savanah is a 22-year-old female was referred to us by the help team due to her case manager reporting that Savanah has been going through significant medication changes since the end of Dec. 2017 and has been experiencing an increase in paranoia and hallucinations. Case manager reports that Savanah has been experiencing people screaming at her and had thoughts about her co-worker being possessed. Case manager also reported that Savanah recently started going to college and was working but, both have been negatively impacted by her increase of symptoms and this medication change. Savanah reports she communicated with her provider on 1/17/18 in which they changed her medication. During the meeting she stated, "I feel pretty good right now. I did not drive my car here, so the demons didn't come with me. I took a taxi so they couldn't follow me here." Savanah recognizes the need for ongoing mental health services. Savanah reports that she has been hospitalized four times since she was 18 with her most recent at New Ulm in August 2017. Savanah reports a significant amount of visual and auditory hallucinations. Savanah reports that she has seen orbs that float around her house and follow her in the community. She reports that these orbs will manifest into beings that can inhabit people's bodies and will become possessed. Savanah also reports that she has been hearing messages that are directed toward her through the television. Savanah states, "I was at work and saw a lady that I knew had become possessed because of the way she was looking at me." She also reports having obsessive thoughts about her paranoid thoughts of people watching her and trying to sabotage her. Savanah reports that she has these thoughts frequently and at times requires assistance from her husband to challenge these thoughts. Savanah states, "Sometimes I have to call him from work, and he helps me get through it." Due to an increase of symptoms Savanah has had to leave work early and has been calling into work. She has not been completing her online schooling and has not been leaving the house if at all possible. Admission is supported at this time due to the increase in voices and medication changes impacting her ability to feel safe in the community. Without intervention Savanah may require a higher level of care.

January 18th 2018

There are so many things going on right now. I am worried about the particle people and that they won't find me at home and instead wait at my house to attack when I come home. Usually they hide with me and follow my car, but I took a taxi to the crisis facility, so they may not have followed. It leaves them to be home with Mitchel. I'm sure he will be safe they won't swallow him up. He isn't the one they want but could use that to get to me here and attack.

January 18th 2019 – Crisis Facility Staff

Savanah spent a lot of the shift in the living room, sitting quietly or conversing with peers. She did have an episode of nausea and dizziness, that she related to her re-starting Seroquel. Savanah met with staff. Her husband visited and brought her a sweatshirt and slippers. She came to staff can reported she could hear people talking outside of the living room. Staff checked and could not see anybody. The blinds were closed which seemed to alleviate some of her anxiety. Savanah went to bed early. She was sleeping on 8, 9, and 11pm rounds.

January 19th 2018

The particle people are worse than the black figures because they wait until it's dark to come out and are going to swallow and tear me apart. The invisible men know I was doing well, and they took my vulnerability and now take charge.

January 19th 2018 – Crisis Facility Staff

Savanah was out on the unit shortly after the shift began. She had a long night of feeling paranoid and was thankful to her peers and staff for being understanding and helpful. For example, she nearly refused her medication this evening because one of the medications came from a different manufacturer and looked different than it usually does. She was

shown both bottles, allowed to read them and reassured that it was the same medication… She then stated, "Nobody put anthrax in it right?" and took the medication. She also thought she saw shadow people in the bushes outside the window and her peers brought her to staff. Staff and her peers shut the blinds so she would feel comfortable continuing to watch the movie with them. Savanah ate with her peers, had 1:1 with staff, and attended evening reflections. She reported she intended to let go of "the paranoid thoughts, I couldn't" and that her world would be "amazing" if she could let go of it forever. She shared her emotion is "paranoid/confused" and rated her mood as a 5 out of 10.

Symptoms: **Savanah had a difficult evening struggling with her paranoid thoughts, but at the same time is aware and able to verbalize that they are "just my paranoia". She shared with her peers and they have been understanding.**

January 20th 2018 – Stay at the Crisis Facility

The doors are locked but I am skeptical. They don't know what they are going up against. There are beasts in the darkness. Right now, I feel on edge I have the feeling people are coming to swarm the building. The doorbell makes me uneasy because I do not know the people coming in whether they are here to harm me. I have the feeling of people watching me. Something bad is going to happen but I'm not sure what yet.

January 20th 2018 – Crisis Facility Staff

Savanah was in the dining room watching television with peers when staff arrived. She then walked with staff and peers over to Walgreens. When she returned, she ate dinner. After dinner she met 1.1 with staff. She then watched television in the dining room with peers. She independently presented for her medications around 7pm and actively participated in evening reflections stating, "I learned that I am not alone." She then had a snack and went to bed. She was seen in the dining room an hour later stating, "I just don't want to be in my room alone." She later went back to her room. She is currently in her room. Symptoms: Savanah reported feeling 'worried, anxious, sad and like a failure'. She also

reported her mood a 5/10. Savanah was noted to be tending to internal stimuli throughout the evening.

January 21ˢᵗ 2018 Crisis Facility Staff

Savanah was on the unit watching television by herself in the front living room when this began. As the evening progressed and she began to feel better she spent the evening watching the football game with her peers. Savanah ate with her peers, attended evening reflections, reported for her medication without prompting and had 1:1 staff. Savanah reported today the things she was able to do differently was "distract myself from thoughts" and it helped by "having a PRN and TV, also quiet time in my room". Savanah reported being grateful for "my husband and support system" and rated her mood 8 out of 10. Savanah is currently in her room for bed. She reported to staff that she was going to attempt to use no night light tonight and only leave her door open. She was encouraged by staff to only do what she is comfortable with and plug her night light back in at any time.

Symptoms: Savanah has a good evening and reported no hallucinations/sightings of the "particle people" tonight and that is why she reported feeling comfortable trying to sleep without her nightlight. The removal of nightlights may have been peer suggestion, but this writer cannot be sure.

January 22ⁿᵈ 2018 – Crisis Facility Staff

Savanah requested a PRN of Zyprexa for anxiety. She said her auditory hallucinations had returned – they are telling her that tonight is the night they are coming to get her. Savanah expressed disappointment. "I was doing so well, I even slept without a night light last night. I get so scared," and she started to cry. Staff offered reassurance and reminded Savanah to let staff know when she was feeling scared and anxious. Peers also provided support and compassion.

January 23rd 2018 – Crisis Facility Staff

Savanah was discharged.

January 24th 2018

Its troubling times tonight. My first full day out of the crisis facility. The anxiety is bad, and I work. I can hear the voices creeping in. One and then two of them. I took a PRN at 2:30 pm. For the hallucinations. I had to go to work and here I am now 9:00 pm. And writing. The TV at work had a familiar voice of the men and women I hear talking about me. Their intention: Sabotage. They want me to fail and send the beings along to watch and report my moves and thoughts. The particle people are gone but I can still feel the presence of darkness. They are coming for me. They have their report I am now home with no protection.

In February 2018 I went to the ER in Mankato's Hospital. I was delusional thinking that the people were possessed and had to check badges to make sure they were who they said they were. I didn't watch TV because the voices were using it as camouflage. I waited to be transferred to Austin to their hospital. I got there in the middle of the night and was brought into my room and I met with Dr. R, who was an amazing doctor.

While being there they did diagnostic tests on me to figure out my diagnosis. Dr. R drew a Venn diagram of the possibilities it could be. With each test another diagnosis was crossed out. Unknown to me that my therapist Missy had already changed it to paranoid schizophrenia. The tests came back to point in that direction.

While there they discontinued my Seroquel and Haldol which left me with Lamictal and Zyprexa. As I became more stable on a higher dose of Zyprexa, they sent me home. I returned to work but still had trouble with the hallucinations and delusional thinking. I thought that my coworkers were possessed and that the invisible people were going to swarm the building.

I would sit rocking back and forth in my chair at my desk with my coworkers asking if I was OK. I always replied, "I'm OK, it'll be OK."

February 20th 2018

This is my first week out of the hospital; my new doctor is nice and straight forward about things. I'm still having problems outside the hospital over the weekend. I had demonic voices come to me and command me to "seek him". I'm not sure what it meant or if it means a new being will reveal itself to me one that is much worse than all the others.

Last night I didn't think Mitchel was real because there was someone inside him. He tried to reassure me, but I didn't know how to make it seem true. The thoughts come back to sabotage, they are trying to ruin my life by infiltrating my home and the people who love me, but there must be a way to know they are real.

March 1st 2018

Today I look back and am reminded of my problems. I had to leave work last night because the voices wouldn't stop. I went blank and couldn't stop them from telling me that I should die. I've been having trouble with depression trying to accept the fact that I have schizophrenia. At work there was a phone call from an anonymous number which called multiple times. When I answered, no one was there and it was brought to my attention that they had placed a tracking device in my brain and were tracking my every move to when I go home.

Today I have to be alone and I am worried that the voices will come again on strong. I'm having trouble not doing what they say. They are terrible. I feel like I can't take any more of this.

The next month, March, I went back Austin for psychiatric help

March 14th 2018

I started work at 4:00 pm. I can feel my mind slowly sinking back down into another episode. The paranoia won't subside, it's a constant battle in my brain. One moment I'm good and able to work, and the next I'm worried that a patient will be an invisible person whose body has been taken over.

The tracker inside my brain is blinking. I can feel the signal getting stronger with the electrical signals. The tracker is releasing toxins into my body. I can feel them as my body pulses. How do I rid my body of the toxins or stop the tracker pulsating signals out to the people?

Tomorrow I meet with my case manager and therapist. They will need to know about the tracker and the toxins in my blood. The people that follow me from my home and work; I can feel them waiting for me. They are out to get me and will do anything to fulfill the prophecy. They know I am bad and will need to be taken care of. I'm worried about the possibility of a physical assault by the beings who take over people like vessels.

March 15ᵗʰ 2018

I was sent back to Austin. This time was different. I stayed there from March 15ᵗʰ to April 9ᵗʰ 2018. The doctor had me diagnosed with schizophreniform but soon changed it to paranoid schizophrenia.

The difference between the two is the timeline of symptoms. Schizophreniform is an episode lasting from six months or under whereas Schizophrenia is an episode six months or longer. While there I got help to file for disability and get my student loans forgiven since I could no longer work.

The forms the doctor filled out showed me how truly ill I was and helped me understand that I am unable to work or go to college. This illness is debilitating. The doctor didn't feel comfortable sending me home because we tried it another time and failed.

Which brings me to the next step in recovery. Staying at the IRTS (Intensive Residential Treatment Services) and quitting my job – over the phone.

They were understanding about it and wished me luck in my journey through recovery. While at the hospital in March I had constant voices and visions. It got to the point where I believed that the staff were trying to take my life.

I had command voices telling me to harm the staff because they took my information on paper and from my blood. I believed that since they had all my information, they were going to kill me. I also had visual hallucinations where I saw blood running down the walls and was told that it was a warning sign telling me that the staff had killed others and I was next. The voices also told me that I would be shown who was boss and that I would be condemned and that I am unworthy of love, life, and food.

Chapter Six

The Start of Recovery

April 9th 2018 is when I started my three months stay at the IRTS. I didn't think that I needed to be there. I thought I was better.

April 11th 2018 – Entry by the IRTS Staff for a Progress Note

Around 11:35pm staff was sitting upstairs and heard what sounded like a client crying downstairs. Staff decided to go downstairs and saw Savanah sitting at a table alone and was crying. Staff sat down by Savanah and asked what was wrong. The two other staff members that were working the evening shift were approaching the table. Savanah turned around looked at staff and abruptly sat up and started to scream about something trying to harm her. Savanah appeared to be in distress, scared, and was loudly screaming. She then tried to run but slowed down when she had to get around a staff member that was standing in her path. Staff was able to approach Savanah, ask her to sit in a chair that was provided. Staff used distraction techniques with Savanah. She was asked to say that she was in a safe place and to touch the wall. Savanah kept repeating that she was a 'good girl' and she 'was safe'. This appeared to work for a couple minutes and then she started to say something was trying to harm her and appeared to be scared as evident by her whole body shaking, her eyes were wide and was trying to stand up. Staff again used grounding techniques. Savanah responded to the grounding techniques and immediately stated she was cold and asked for a drink of water. Staff provided her with a blanket and water. Staff then asked Savanah if she wanted to go and sit in the dining area. Savanah was agreeable to the idea.

She ended up sitting in the dining area with staff until she reported that she wanted to go to her room and lay down. Staff asked Savanah if she was suicidal and she reported no.

April 12th 2018 – IRTS STAFF

Writer checked in with Savanah regarding the events of last night. Savanah reported that she has not experienced anything like that before. She talked about experiencing "all the voices at once", suddenly. She reported that she did not understand what happened and that she does not remember exactly what happened. She shared concerns that people would be disappointed in her because she has been doing well. She apologized several times that it happened and that she could not explain exactly what happened. Writer assured her no one was upset with her and that staff just wanted to help. She reported that grounding practices were helpful and that she would.

April 16th 2018 – IRTS STAFF

Client approached staff after group and reported she is hearing 2-3 voices and that they keep chatting back and forth. She repeatedly apologized for not being able to participate in group this morning but states she was unable due to voices. Client states she is afraid someone is going to "come in here and kill everyone with mental health problems". She states the voices had gone away for a while and she doesn't understand why they are back. She stated she's feeling very paranoid and just needs to hold it together until therapy. She says she is glad she's not taking a cab because she's sure someone would kill her. She also talks about being happy that the only ones who know she's here are her parents because she doesn't want the computer to store her information. Client speaks rapidly and is staring at the floor while telling staff about her voices and paranoia. She stated she is going to listen to music but sits by a peer in the dining area to wait for staff to drive her to therapy in a half hour.

April 19th 2018 – IRTS STAFF

Shortly after evening group was over, Savanah approached writer in the medication office. She asked, "Who opened the door to my room? I don't like the door open because I don't know who went in there and went through the stuff. Someone could get into my Chap-stick and put something in there to make me have some sort of reaction or they could pour chemicals all over my blankets!" Writer explained to Savanah that staff may not have latched her door when cueing her for group and apologized. Writer explained that the nurse was not in group and would have seen if someone went into her bedroom. Savanah responded, "OK, sorry, I wasn't trying to be rude."

May 2nd 2018 – IRTS STAFF

Shortly before supper this writer observed Savanah standing alone in the dining area murmuring something. When writer approached Savanah, this writer heard Savanah repeating, "Savanah stay good..." When this writer asked Savanah if she was OK, Savanah stated that she was having trouble with "the voices" and that she was especially terrified of the "big voice". Savanah stated she was receiving messages and command from the television that was on in the dining area and that "everyone" was conspiring against her. Savanah further stated that she would be unable to control herself if she were to receive commands "from the big voice". Savanah stated she was having a bad day and that loud stimulation was making her symptoms worse. This writer assured Savanah that she was in a safe place and encouraged her to find a quieter place if she felt that would help decrease her symptoms and focus on the present moment. Savanah went to her room after this writer assured her that the television in the dining area would be turned off during mealtime. Savanah later ate supper with her peers without incident and stated that she would try and attend evening meeting and excuse herself if her symptoms became more acute.

May 2nd 2018 – IRTS STAFF

Writer was walking by the upstairs office when another mental health practitioner, A. asked writer to step – into the office where she and Savanah were sitting. Practitioner explained that Savanah was having a lot of symptoms. Savanah talked about hearing a voice earlier before group and being unsure if it was a real voice but thinking it sounded like the "man voice" that she hears and that will tell her to do things. She appeared quite anxious. She would talk about her concerns that she will have to get a med change if she tells staff of her symptoms or that others will be disappointed in her and then she would talk under her breath stating, "No Savanah, you are OK," or, "they are not coming." Writer and staff suggested that Savanah try to focus on the present moment. Savanah identified that maybe eating a banana and having hot chocolate would help. Practitioner A asked Savanah if she would like to sit with the nurse as the rest of staff had a meeting to attend. Savanah stated this would be OK. She became frightened while approaching the stairs, but Savanah was able to take some assistance from staff and to talk herself down. Writer had Savanah sit in writer's office with the nurse. Writer got a picture for Savanah to color. After staff meeting writer checked in again and she stated she was feeling better after watching funny videos with the nurse about singer tryouts. She stated she felt well enough to sit in the dining room and color. She agreed she would check in with staff if symptoms increased again.

May 4th 2018 – IRTS STAFF

Savanah was sitting in evening reflections when she turned around and looked at staff and said, "They are coming to get me." Staff assisted Savanah with leaving the conference room and went out to the patio to assist Savanah by using grounding techniques and distractions. Savanah was able to ground herself and she reported that her symptoms decreased. She reported that she has experienced an increase in stress, and she contributes the increase in hallucinations due to stress. She shared that she is hoping that she can maintain her mental health symptoms with her current medications and dosages.

May 6th 2018 – IRTS STAFF

Writer chit chatted with client this morning about how her evening went with her family. She stated that they went to Applebee's and she had a very good time. She became paranoid once when staff was moving tables around thinking that they were blocking her in to come and get her, but her family was able to ground her, talking her through it, showing her that if they needed to leave which route they would be able to take. She states that she is very fortunate that she has a family who are so supportive of her and know how to help her through rather than telling her that she is embarrassing them. She is super excited about going home with her husband today and hanging out, cleaning and helping him get ready for the week.

May 10th 2018 – IRTS STAFF

Writer found client in the dining room staring off at nothing, writer sat with client as client told writer that client began to watch a movie about aliens with her peers but that an alien appeared, spoke the written word and then spit acid on the actors in the movie. Client stated she found this to be too overwhelming and left the movie. Client grounded herself by telling herself out loud that it was just a movie, that the alien was fake and that the alien will NOT come out of the TV and get her. Client sat with writer and talked about lighter things in life then presented for meds, again talking lightly and laughing with staff members. Client stated she felt better and was going to her room to read something before going to sleep.

May 11th 2018 – IRTS STAFF

At 2:00am Friday morning, Savanah approached this writer in the downstairs staff office and asked if she had missed group. Writer explained that it was 2:00 in the morning and asked if everything was OK or if Savanah would like talk about something. Savanah responded, "No, I just thought I was taking a nap and missed group." Savanah then returned to her room. Writer will continue to monitor and chart accordingly.

May 11th 2018 – IRTS STAFF

Writer approached Savanah because she was walking in a small circle outside of her bedroom door. Savanah appeared to be responding to internal stimuli, stating, "No, Savanah. They can't get through the wood door," over and over. Writer encouraged Savanah to make a cup of tea and sit with writer in the dining area. Savanah began to make a cup of tea but had to stop the microwave because "it's ticking away at my life". Writer continually reminded Savanah, "Your brain tells you they're real, but they aren't real." She became tearful several times while sitting with writer. Savanah gradually grounded herself and stated that she was going to try to go back to bed and would find writer if the voices continued.

May 18th 2018

10:30am after self-esteem group. The electrical signals were checking in with me right away after I woke up. The realization to be free again. Kill the computer man. He holds the key to my freedom. I think back to the image that I was given. I look for clues but I'm coming up empty. Who is this brown-haired man? Who will join me in my fight for myself?

Soon my brain needs to be destroyed to begin again – anew. Who is the man and why does he want control over me? He needs to die. No switch flipping. I'm trying to sleep but the thoughts and visions creep in. He turns in his chair and he has no face, just a blur. Is my mind trying to protect me? He's keeping my life's secrets from me.

The voices are back and active talking bad about me. I will be nothing, you will die, it's over, you are gone, they say. The voices calling me with their lies. Their deceit is what gives them power. They feed on my fear. I want to be left alone. Someone will die in the house tonight. It may be me. I've seen the blood on my hands. Washed clean at supper. The war will come tonight. I am amped up to prepare for the fight.

The Computer Man

Chaos Forever

He will bring hell fro

This is the image of the computer man who appeared to me first at Austin hospital and then continued to visit me at the IRTS. I believe he was open to coming to the IRTS to finish me off. My mind portrayed "the beast" who would drag out the dead bodies after the computer man, the man with no face, would set fire to the building killing all of us unless I stopped him.

May 19ᵗʰ 2018 – Level 6 Somewhat Difficult

I struggled today with the thoughts of the computer man. The pass went well until we got to Applebee's. I tried to ground myself but there was too much going on. I was trying to be rational. People with earpieces were just waiters and not people to harm me or put things in my brain. I believe they are all plotting against me. I came back feeling a bit 'off'. I went to bed at 8:00 pm. Mitchel helped ground me with the sugar packets and talk through my problems.

May 20ᵗʰ 2018

I awoke from my nap feeling 'off'. Something doesn't feel right, I feel like my life is a ruse of some sort. A fake reality being controlled by a person like a mouse in a maze or a marionette doll. I try to ground but can't shake the feeling. Something is wrong, people play their roles. How do I know who is a true person? I reach out for help and we go for a walk.

The outside is scary – every building is a clay model, and if I were to touch, it would squish between my fingers. I'm so confused. Has the life I lived been a game for the computer man? Will he take the joy away from me and put me in the circle of despair, a false belief? Why does my mind do this? Is it slowly reaching its claws past the drape over my eyes, trying to get me to see the reality of nothing? All this time I have loved and lost and now it's close to permanent loss. I feel I'm becoming too aware for the computer man and he will slowly take my life away. They are placing bets on my life.

May 20ᵗʰ 2018 – IRTS STAFF

Savanah approached staff to inform them that she was having thoughts that she was part of a SIM game and that someone or something was controlling her movements. Staff asked Savanah if she wanted to go outside for a walk and to use grounding techniques. Savanah was open to going out for a walk. Savanah and staff walked around the building and identified what she could see, smell, hear, and touch. Savanah reported that everything appeared that it was made of clay. She was able to identify

seeing a lilac tree and reported it reminded her of spring and she then touched the grass. She then stated that she wanted to go to her room to write a poem. Staff went inside with her and later and shared that she wanted to draw a picture for staff of how the IRTS building looked to her and who was controlling everybody at the IRTS and that nothing is real. Staff asked her to try some more grounding techniques with them such as holding ice in her hand. Savanah was open to trying the technique. She sat with staff and held ice in both of her hands. She reported how the ice felt. This appeared to have helped Savanah as evidenced by her not talking about the computer man and her being controlled. Dinner arrived and Savanah remained in the dining room and ate with her peers. She went to her room after dinner and wrote a poem which she ended up sharing with staff.

May 21ˢᵗ 2018 – Bed Time at 6:00 pm

Today was a good day in the beginning, then group came. As I sit, they are across from me planting thoughts and sending messages to each other and back to the computer man. I'm not sure if he knows where I am but the premonition of him has been shown, so now is the waiting game. The staff assured me they would know if evil spirits are here, they can tell. I hope that is the truth. They will protect me overnight. I feel like there are cameras in the TV sending me messages. I want to watch TV but the electrical signals being pushed on my brain are too much to handle.

May 21ˢᵗ 2018 – IRTS STAFF

Savanah approached this writer several times throughout the evening sharing that she was struggling with her thoughts that the "computer man is going to come and flip the switch". Savanah reported that she felt that her peers were gaining up on her during evening reflections by trying to poison her pen or poisoning her through her air vents. Savanah also reported that she was hearing command voices that were telling her to harm others. Savanah then kept repeating that she "doesn't want to hurt others" and that she is a "good person". Staff utilized several grounding techniques such as drinking hot tea to help distract Savanah from the voices. Staff utilized reflective listening when meeting with Savanah.

May 22ⁿᵈ 2018

This morning people were staring at me I could feel them watching, putting stuff in my brain. I'm struggling with the thoughts of commands – that they will take over tonight. Group is going OK. I am calm right now. I hear the noises coming to get me. They are going to set the building on fire and the computer man will control the beast to drag out the bodies. He wants me to die, leave all the people alone and I can suffer. I don't want to hurt anyone. I will be OK.

May 22ⁿᵈ 2018 – IRTS STAFF

Writer checked in with Savanah to see how she was doing and see if she was interested in going to the crisis facility. Savanah was sitting at a dining room table singing to herself that she is OK and that she only needs to make it to her appointment tomorrow. Savanah identified that she was struggling with the voices that none of her coping strategies (drinking hot tea, coloring, playing with Play-Doh) aren't currently working to lessen them. She stated that she has had some auditory command hallucinations telling her to harm herself or harm others, Savanah stated that she has been telling the voices to shut up and leave her alone and that she will not harm herself or others. She has been sitting with staff in the dining room as this is helping her to feel safe. Savanah declined the offer to go to the crisis facility but stated, "If I change my mind, I will let staff know." The crisis facility had been informed of the situation and told staff will call if the need increases. Savanah has stated she feels safe at the IRTS and that she will continue to try coping strategies and then will go to bed early. Savanah is currently on 30min checks.

May 24ᵗʰ 2018

They are trying to get my information by asking questions and watching me. They are taking notes to give out. I was in group and there was some type of perfume disguising the poison. I was going to cough it up, but they shut the door. I feel like I need to fight for control over my mind. I need to overcome and be ready for the war. Will I have people to back me up?

> *Evil beings*
> *War*
> *Computer man*
> *Not real life*

May 27th 2018

They talk about evil as if they know what it is. I've seen evil before my eyes in the dark figures and computer man. They do now know what they are talking about. They are inviting them in by addressing it. They have been taken over and are working against me.

I stay in my room trying to be safe away from them. I can hear them inside waiting to be unleashed. I'm OK for the moment. I now know what to do. Should I lock my door and wait for it to pass? How long will I have to wait for it to be clear again? Do I reach out? Do I speak or try to sleep again? I am unsure.

They do not know that power they possess. It will soon be shown to me the future of myself in this place. I am an evil person up to no good. I am bad and undeserving. Have I killed someone? Taking over my dreams are nightmares. Nothing is the same. The reality unfamiliar. I tried to sleep it off, but nothing is helping.

I am reminded in my subconscious that I am evil, there is nothing for me. I should not eat because they tell me I don't deserve food. It is poison waiting to kill me. Payback for what I have done – I will try and eat because my stomach is hungry. Do I dare go against my brain and fight for control? I tried to eat most of my meal, but it got difficult. What the voices tell me: You think you know what evil is? I'll show you. You will be stripped of everything you know and love. You will be and are nothing. No one finds you desirable. You are undeserving. You are no good. You do not deserve food or water. You do not deserve love. No relationships. No health. You are gone. Done. Over with. No one will stop us from destroying you. We will break you down. You have lost. You cannot overcome us. We are in control. There is no way out. You are stuck with us. We are forever.

This was a picture that I drew about the aura I would see around people that showed me they were not real people. It was difficult to look past it, but I tried.

May 28th 2018 – IRTS STAFF

Savanah approached staff and asked if she could talk, she shared that she was struggling and was hearing voices and paranoia. Savanah and staff went for a walk but had to return after 2 blocks due to Savanah thinking that people were "tracking" her. Staff and Savanah returned to the IRTS to have a glass of hot tea. Savanah started to say out loud that she was a "bad person" and that someone is "controlling her". When the nurse brought her medications, Savanah then kept repeating that she thinks someone is trying to "poison" her. Savanah did end up taking her medications after staff reassured her that she is in a safe place. Staff also utilized distraction and grounding techniques. Savanah completed her glass of hot tea and then shared she wanted to go to bed due to her brain being "exhausted".

May 29th 2018

It started in the morning again with electrical signals from TV's, phones, and computers. They are trying to knock in my brain. The wall is up. They do not understand the severity of the security compromise. They go about their day. I've warned them that the computer man is behind everything – he's the one making my meds not work. He is in control. These decisions are not mine to be made. The computer man is coming for me today. No free will.

May 29th 2018 – IRTS STAFF

Writer was asked to intervene during a conversation Savanah Boike was having with another MH practitioner. When writer approached, Savanah was pacing in a small office muttering words at a rapid pace about the computer man and how he is going to find her. She said staff are sharing information about people and communicating with her doctor and "staff needed to know how serious this is". Savanah was staring at the floor while she paced and did not appear to be blinking. Savanah, writer, and her point staff then went into Savanah's bedroom where she said she felt safe because the "being" couldn't get through her door. Savanah

continued to mutter about her delusions and breathing heavily. She practiced deep breathing exercises and was able to recognize objects in her room to keep her grounded. Writer suggested the hospital to Savanah and initially she became even more anxious and stated she would not go there. At this point another practitioner was brought in where they explained that going to the hospital would help with medication change and would also be a safe place to stay. Savanah said she felt like a failure for going back there. Savanah then called her husband, Mitchel with staff present to inform him that she would be going to the hospital. Writer contacted ED social worker to inform her Savanah would be on her way up with staff and told her about all the recent symptoms Savanah has been experiencing. She was informed that Savanah would need a medication change and cannot be managed at the IRTS facility at this time.

May 30ᵗʰ 2018

I feel uneasy today like something bad is going to happen. I feel the electrical signals again. I feel like my brain is not my own it is separate from me. The feelings of being attacked are active. The chattering voices slowly calling my name. They say they know what evil is.

I'll show them! I am the savior of the IRTS. I will challenge the computer man when he comes. I need to fight him for control of my body and brain. I felt the shaking of the building – a sign he is coming to get me. I told staff they need to lock the doors and form a barricade until I can finally save them from the computer man. I feel it rise deep inside, the power to overcome. A snap of my fingers and he is gone. Only for short. I need to find a more permanent solution – he must die! He must be taken away. I have to be the protector. The savior to the IRTS people. The man with no face – the computer man.

May 30ᵗʰ 2018 – IRTS STAFF

Savanah exhibited symptoms of psychosis at times throughout the evening. Savanah primarily focused on a fixed delusion that "the computer man" was attempting to invade the building and she stated that she "…needed to protect everyone from the computer man…". Savanah would at times insist that only she had the power to protect everyone from the computer man. At one time Savanah stated that her room was shaking violently and that the "tiles are moving around". Savanah also expressed feeling some irritability due to staffs' inability to observe the delusions she was experiencing and said that staff do not "understand the danger…". Staff reassured Savanah that she was in a safe place and redirected her to center herself by interacting with and focusing on a real object such as the one of the tension balls she purchased recently and/or listen to music. Savanah stated that was effective to some degree and is currently trying to relax in her room.

May 31st 2018 – IRTS STAFF

Around 6:20 pm Savanah came running to the med room stating, "They are coming to get me! I saw their feet under my door, I think they can get through my door now, they are coming." Writer explained to Savanah that "they" are not real and asked Savanah to use some grounding skills, writer asked her to touch the wall and look at writer to think about positive affirmations like Savanah's therapist suggested. Writer escorted Savanah to her room as Savanah stated that she could get her squishy toy. Writer again explained to Savanah that there was nothing there, that Savanah was safe. Writer sat with Savanah in the dining room while Savanah utilized her squishy toy to ground herself. Savanah did write down some positive affirmations as well but her first one was "the voices are liars" and Savanah became very upset reading this one stating, "I should not have written that, now I have provoked them they are really mad at me now! If I die tonight it is because of the computer man, because of them coming to get me!" Savanah was able to ground herself again with the squishy toy and then told writer what she would do if she were at home which would be to take her meds and go to bed. Writer confirmed with Savanah twice that Savanah felt safe taking her meds and go to bed since it was close to 7pm. Savanah agreed and stated she did feel better and that she was very tired. Writer gave meds at 6:55pm and Savanah went to bed. Savanah told writer she will be locking her door this evening and asked that this be passed to the night shift as well and she again told writer to pass on to staff that if she dies it's because of the computer man.

June 1st 2018 – IRTS STAFF

Writer met with Savanah in writer's office after she left the PEP group this afternoon. She was hyper-verbal stating that they are out to get everyone and that they "the invisible people and computer man" were gassing out her and her peers while in group. She stated that they were tapping on the walls trying to break them down to get her. She continues to have thoughts that "they" have taken place in her peers' bodies and that they are going to harm herself and other peers and that she needs to make a plan to keep herself and others safe. Another practitioner and writer provided feedback that everyone is safe here with staff here 24/7 and cameras we know who is coming in and out of the buildings. Practitioner had Savanah play with Play-Doh to move around in her hands. Savanah stated again that she needs to either create a map or a time frame so that we can figure out who took/murdered her when she is gone. She reported that she has one PRN to take but does not want to take it until later in the afternoon so she is unsure how she will cope now. She stated that she is trying her coping strategies (squishy ball) and telling herself that she is in control and that they cannot control her. She stated that Mitchel, her husband, is going to come visit her today and tomorrow. She stated that she is also going to try and finish cleaning her bedroom, vacuum and dust. She requested to also go to Family Dollar to find some Ensure or Boost as she has no motivation to eat but continues to be hungry.

June 1st 2018 – IRTS STAFF

Writer sat in the dining area with Savanah for a while this morning. She reported that she was going to try and stay out of her room today because she is tired of trying to sleep and there is too much noise from other people. Writer provided positive feedback and encouragement that she is safe in this facility and she can feel safe in common areas. She stated that she will do her best in that she still believes that some of her peers are working with the computer man at this time. She stated because she feels so tired from her medication, she has difficulty chewing and swallowing drier foods. She reported that she has ramen noodles in her storage box

71

to eat if she cannot eat lunch this afternoon. Savanah reported that she feels bad that she is not participating in the program since she is not currently attending groups. She stated that she has a strong work ethic and it makes it difficult to not attend the groups at this time. Writer offered positive reinforcement that she is working hard at this time managing her symptoms that she should not have to go into a situation (groups) that is going to increase those symptoms from occurring at this time.

June 1ˢᵗ 2018 – IRTS STAFF

Savanah approached the IRTS staff office and stated there are people who got into her bedroom and are poisoning her through her vents. She stated she had to leave her bedroom because she's being gassed. Writer reassured her that she is safe in her bedroom and that nobody is going to hurt her. Eventually she replied, "okay" and went to sit at the dining room tables.

June 2ⁿᵈ/3ʳᵈ 2018

The invisible people are here waiting outside my door. The computer man watching. It's been shown he is in a warehouse but not sure where. It could be somewhere in Mankato.

I posted signs on my door so while he is watching through the cameras, he knows I know he's watching me. It also serves as a warning sign for other clients, so they know the invisible people are here too. They are plotting against me. I hear their thoughts through electrical signals. The cameras will show the truth behind everyone. They are wearing masks to hide their evil. I sit, sit, sit, back and forth listening for the quiet that will come.

The voices are too much. I have to get out of here. I am no longer safe, only in my room. I do not know what to do. Everything is overpowering. I feel over stimulated so many things going on at once. Everyone is evil. They wait their turn. I made my presence known. That I know they are after me with the signs on the door. The other people know not what evil they are capable of. They will use their powers against me. What powers do I have?

The warehouse was shown to me. The staff do not know where it is located. I'm getting closer to finding the computer man.

The computer man will be no match for me once I find out my superpowers. I will be free soon. I will kill the computer man in the battle here at the IRTS. I will gather more people to fight the invisible people. I wonder if I am a medium and all the things I have been shown were meant for a specific people or reason. Maybe he is keeping my dad there at the warehouse and he didn't really die. I am the savior for everyone. The staff are now aware of the warehouse and computer man. Hopefully we will be able to locate him, so I can survive the day and night.

June 2nd 2018 – IRTS STAFF

Savanah took her morning meds at 8:00am and writer gave the Haldol PRN at 8:30am as Savanah came to the med room mumbling about electrical signals coming from the TV and how she has to warn all of us. Savanah stated that the electrical signals are controlling the ones whose bodies have been taken over by the bad ones. She went on to state, "If anything happens to me, it is the bad people, tell everyone so they know who did it." Savanah decided to get her own ear buds and listen to music in the dining room while the TV was on.

June 3rd 2018 – IRTS STAFF

Savanah asked for her PRN at 8:30am, writer asked her to try practicing other coping skills first since she just took her scheduled meds 30 minutes ago. Savanah apologized profusely for asking for the PRN but agreed to the idea of trying other coping skills, she did return at 10:30am for the PRN. Savanah stated she was getting triggered by a client talking about electrical signals and again by the dishwasher staff talking/singing out loud while working, and she also asked the writer if she even needs to take medication at all, that "maybe it's the medication that is making these things happen". Savanah also came to staff asking if we could hear the sirens too, but there were no sirens. At lunch Savanah froze while walking to a table with her food and began whispering, this writer asked Savanah to sit down and eat and notice the food, the taste and texture.

Savanah began to eat and stated she would be fine. Writer observed Savanah to eat her entire meal and she went to her room.

This is the warehouse where I believe the computer man to be living. I was unsure of where it was located but I was shown it is either Mankato or the cities.

June 3ʳᵈ 2018 – IRTS STAFF

Savanah ate supper after everyone else was done, because she stated there were too many people. Savanah was excused from the evening meeting because she stated there were too many people and electronics putting thoughts into her mind. Savanah later approached writer with two drawings, one was what she called "the warehouse where the computer

man was at and this one is what the computer man looks like". Savanah stated that she thinks, "Maybe someone is trying to send me a message, maybe it's my dad." Savanah stated, "I saw my dad die and he is cremated but maybe this was all a trick and the computer man has him and he wants me to save him." Savanah stated, "We have to get an army together and find the computer man, before he comes to set this place on fire and destroy us all."

Writer reassured Savanah that she will be safe here and that staff are here to help her and make sure everyone is safe Savanah stated, "That's good," and returned to her room.

June 4th 2018 – IRTS STAFF

Savanah requested to speak with writer this morning. She requested if writer wants to read the poem that she wrote over the weekend. She reported that she also has done some drawings of the beings and other things she sees. She went to her room and came back with a journal and three-ring binder. She read her poem to writer on her 'it is' poem on her experience with Schizophrenia. She also shared what the vessels that take over her peers look like to Savanah. (they have a red aura around their head and have a green mask over their eyes, the also do not have a mouth as they do not speak). She also drew the invisible people vs. her and her peers stating that a war is going to happen at the IRTS, and she is the only one that can save everyone but has not figured out how she can do that at this time. Savanah reported she plans on bringing her drawings (including the one of the computer man and also the warehouse which she believes he is currently staying in) to ask her doctor if she has seen either one of them. Savanah reported that if she can find out if anyone has seen this warehouse or where it is located, she can send authorities to it and get the computer man. She is worried that her doctor is going to completely take her off her current medications and start her on all new ones. Writer provided positive feedback that she will get changes but there will be titrations for both decreasing and increasing them. She thanked writer for talking and left writer's office.

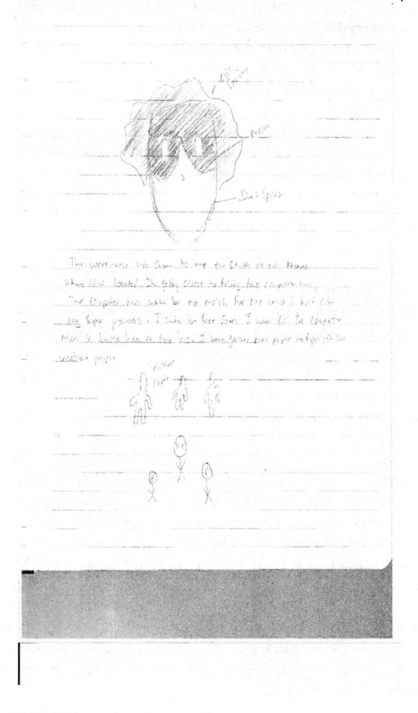

The invisible people are portrayed here as the "wiggly" people. They were always watching waiting to give their repot back to the one who was in control.

While being sick I found myself seeing the fake people or imposters they had a green mask and a red aura around them. It was an easy tell for me.

June 4th 2018

Another client is asking me for information on which clinic I go to for my psychiatrist and Mitchel's middle name. I feel like she's working with the staff and computer man.

June 5th 2018 – IRTS STAFF

Writer noticed Savanah crying at the med room door and speaking in a loud voice to another staff member. Writer encouraged Savanah to come to the team room to get away from all the supper times commotion. Savanah stated two other clients were "plotting against" her and they were "slandering" her name. Writer continually reassured Savanah that she was safe and that she did not need to worry about what other peers were doing. Savanah ate supper in the team room with writer. She began smacking the top of her head saying, "Leave me alone! I just want to eat!" She told writer that she will not hurt anyone "unless I am provoked first". Writer completed several grounding exercises with Savanah, which appeared to ease her symptoms some. She went outside with writer and noticed the other client was also outside. She stated and kept repeating an unrecognizable phrase that contained the words "body, mind, ignite". Savanah stated she was going to call and talk to her husband in her room. Writer walked her to her bedroom and encouraged her to come to staff if needed.

June 5th 2018

10:00am I took my PRN about two hours ago. The electrical signals are present right away this morning. They bombarded me coming from all directions trying to infiltrate my brain. I'm not sure why or what they want except to get in and plant evil thoughts.

June 6th 2018

I woke up this morning to electrical signals and the chattering voices. The voices sit there and talk about me. I started to cry because I want peace. Hopefully the new med will come today. I don't know how much longer I can take this. I feel like I want to die so my brain can rest forever – and it wants to take me with it.

June 6th 2018 – IRTS STAFF

Writer checked in with Savanah a number of times during the day shift. Savanah would talk about her delusions and then talk about how she "couldn't take this anymore" and her "brain hurt". Writer went for a short walk with Savanah after lunch to try and give her a break from so many people talking, get some sunshine and try to ground her in a new setting. Savanah talked with writer throughout the walk and did not bring up her delusions. She did talk about her overwhelming feelings of hopelessness. Several times today when talking to writer, Savanah started to cry. Writer validated and empathized with Savanah's feelings.

June 7th 2018

I am the savior of here and thought I should do rounds to ensure patient safety. I do NOT have schizophrenia. It is due to unseen forces. This is a false reality. Nothing is safe or free. I must have all of this happen because I'm on my cycle. It has nothing to do with my brain.

I am the savior of the broken. Here in this false reality I am queen. The computer man is playing tricks with me. We will all be OK. One day I will find the truth and reality in life. The walls are paper thin, hollow, no roof only the maze. We will all be OK. I am here and in control. I'm fighting the electrical signals with my music. It helps send other messages outweighing the others.

I met with Mitchel today. We had a good visit. He tried to reassure me that this is reality, but I still can't let go of the thought of false reality – a fallen world soon to be judged. Who will judge? Who am I to be?

I'm going to be OK. I am in control. How to prove what must I do? I don't feel OK even though I try to portray I am. My reality is so unforgiving and always changing. Nothing set in stone. I feel alone. Trapped in a reality not my own.

I feel I'm crumbling underneath the weight of the world. The constant worrying between realities. How do I tell what is real? I feel there is no way out except death, but medication will have to suffice. Not a permanent solution but soon to be better.

It just takes time Savanah. You will get better – time is ticking – wasting away on what could be helping. Savanah, death is not the answer! Give it time. You will be OK. I know it.

You have bounced back before. The weight will ease off soon. Just try your best is all I ask of you. Just take the time and don't worry about groups. Focus on yourself and get better. No self – harm! You will be OK!

I'd rather take medication than die. My brain is broken. It knows not the severity of this situation it is alternate realities and electrical signals.

He is taking over. Infiltrating the building first with the invisible people/light bringers. Soon to be a war here. They are watching and waiting for their time to strike. How to fight them off? No way. The computer man, man of misery and bad times. I'm so confused I don't know what I am supposed to be doing.

Take your medication! Its only time now!

Death is not the answer! DO NOT CUT! There will be a better life!

I feel like my blood is toxic.

This is a diagram I drew as I felt like that the building was fake, so I found myself looking at it as a sky view trying to figure out which was true. My brain or the staff members who tried to convince me I was safe, and the building was real.

June 7th 2018 – IRTS STAFF

Savanah approached staff in the hallway outside of the nurse's station and reported that she is "hungry" but the voices "won't let me eat. The voices tell me that I'm bad and I don't deserve food". Savanah then became tearful and said, "I wish I was dead." Staff redirected Savanah and asked her if it would help if staff sat with her while she ate. Savanah agreed to sit with staff and try to eat again. Staff prepared Savanah's plate of food and sat with her while she ate. The Mental Health Practitioner was called and informed about Savanah's suicidal statements. The MHP directed staff to find out if she had a plan or intent. Staff approached Savanah and asked her if she had a plan to intent. Savanah stated "no" to both but did state that yesterday she had images of cutting her arms and she said that the image scared her. Savanah promised to be able to remain safe while at the IRTS and will inform staff if she experienced an increase in suicidal thoughts. She also exhibited forward thinking by stating that she needs to wait for the meds to kick in. She told staff that she doesn't want to die. She acknowledged that death is "final". Staff update the MHP and was directed to keep Savanah on half hour checks. Savanah retired to her room after PM meds kicked in and appeared to be resting at 7pm rounds.

June 8th 2018 – IRTS STAFF

Client mentioned to writer that she didn't want to eat her meal last night because the voices were telling her not to and she was afraid there would be "repercussions". Client did not eat breakfast. Writer asked client about lunch, and she was really tired and wanted to rest and wasn't sure if she wanted to eat. After peers were done eating client approached writer wanting to shower. Writer asked if client had eaten today and she said she hadn't. Writer encouraged client to sit and eat something and offered to sit with client. Client reluctantly agreed and did sit with writer and eat 2 meat/cheese on bun sandwiches. Client states the voices and people have been really bad this morning and she had been afraid about all of the people she was seeing around, but states it is a little better now.

Client finishes lunch and goes to take a shower – she reports she hasn't showered since Monday and thinks it will help her feel better.

June 8ᵗʰ 2018 – IRTS STAFF

Savanah reports having difficulty eating meals in the dining area due to her symptoms. Writer presented the option to sit at the small table in the downstairs and eat her meal with a staff member. Savanah ate supper with staff at the table and ate the majority of her meal.

June 10ᵗʰ 2018

4:00 pm: the invisible people have infiltrated the building. I saw one standing in the staircase. As I approached it started to move back. There must be something inside of me that deters them from coming too close.

4:17pm: made around the half of the building. No invisible people outside they must have found a hiding place.

4:41pm: it's getting close to supper time. I'm tired but I have a duty to protect the other people here. One of the beings tried to communicate with me. I told them I can't talk to them. I wish they would understand.

5:20 pm: the other clients are talking and trying to get information out of me with "how are you?" There are monsters who have taken over my music. I hear different voices than the person actually singing.

I'm being trapped in my own head – me – I'm stuck here wondering about these actions. What I'm doing. What I am saying. I am a robot, I am no one. There is no one to help.

- *I am someone else*
- *Some sick person has overtaken*
- *I am not my own person*
- *I am not sick*

I always felt like I was trapped inside my own mind like being a spectator to my own life. I always battled with who would be in control my "normal" self or the illness. And for most of the time it was the illness that won.

June 11th 2018 – *11:35am: there are people in the TV's watching everyone even the computer man. Voices are active.*

June 12th 2018

Today I'm having trouble again. The voices are active and relentless with their chattering. I need to run and leave this place. Maybe if I ran, they would leave me alone. I can't take much more of this – why me?

I am strong, but I feel like the darkness is stronger. My depression worsening. I think about the times I've cut, and it brings back the feeling of release. I have too many emotions and things going on I don't know how to handle it. My two moods now that I deal with is psychosis or depression. It's never ending just constant – persistent.

The building is why the voices are active. I'm very uncomfortable right now with them chattering and other noises to stop.

The voices become more frightening telling me to run and that I will need to do bloodletting.

June 12th 2018 – IRTS STAFF

Writer was sitting in the dining room area charting on a computer when client walked into dining area to get lunch. Client sat down by a peer and ate a sandwich. Client kept turning around to look at writer. Client eventually asked writer if writer was safe being on the computer. Writer assured client that writer was safe. Client then states she wants to run away. She says she just can't handle the voices and if she runs away maybe the voices will stay in the building. Writer explained that voices don't work that way and leaving the building would not free her of them. Writer assured client is in a safe place and staff are here to help. Writer asked client what she does to help when the voices get bad. Client had taken a PRN about 2 hours prior and only has one more dose available for the remainder of the day. Client is in her room at this time. Writer asked client to come find staff if the music is not helpful.

June 12th 2018 – IRTS STAFF

Writer contacted Savanah's case manager regarding the increase of symptoms. Writer informed her staff have been completing 30-minute

checks on Savanah for the past few days and that she is talking about having to leave the facility because she believes there are dead bodies within the walls. Case manager stated she supports anything the IRTS staff have to do to keep her safe. Writer informed all staff that if Savanah were to leave the building staff should call 911 right away.

June 13th 2018

The voices calling my name wanting me to follow them. I'm not sure where to go or what they want from me. The blood lady came today and took my first sample. I'm worried my information has been stolen.

June 14th 2018 – IRTS STAFF

Writer picked up Savanah this afternoon from her individual therapy appointment. She stated that she had a lot of things to talk/reassure herself with staff today. She stated that she is paranoid that staff are plotting to kill her, especially now that she had her blood drawn yesterday and it is getting shipped to California for testing. She stated she has thoughts that staff are going to suffocate her with her pillow but that at this moment there is not writing on the wall yet, so she is unsure if these thoughts are true. Writer validated Savanah's feelings and provided positive reinforcement that staff are here to keep her safe. She reported that she has to make more signs for her room telling her to take medications and that she is safe.

June 15th 2018 – IRTS STAFF

Writer removed Savanah from 30-minute checks at this time. Savanah appears to have moments throughout the day where her thoughts are clearer and she's able to state that she knows the thoughts she is having are her symptoms. Savanah stated if she starts to feel confused, she will find staff right away.

June 15th 2018 – IRTS STAFF

Client approached writer and asked if it was OK to take her PRN. She reports she is seeing the invisible people and they are going to take over this building and we all need to quietly evacuate. She states she has been thinking this all day but has been too tired to do anything about it. Client reports she wants to take a PRN but is too tired and she doesn't know if she should. Writer encouraged client to take her PRN, as she hasn't tried it yet today and she's having delusional thoughts that are upsetting her. Client takes her PRN Haldol and states she is going to lay down.

June 15th 2018

I had trouble at supper tonight the TV's have people inside them watching me, waiting.

June 20th 2018 – IRTS STAFF

Savanah told writer that she has hung signs on the inside of her door that have "really been helping". She reports hanging a stop sign picture that informs her to stop and ask staff what to do if she is confused. Another sign tells her that there "may not be a check point downtown" and that she does not have to listen to her voices. Savanah reports recognizing an improvement since her Clozaril continues to be increased. Writer informed Savanah that staff has also recognized a slight improvement, as she is able to engage in more reality-based conversations throughout the day compared to two to three weeks ago. It also appears Savanah is beginning to again question if her delusions are real or not, as compared to two to three weeks ago when she had intense belief that her delusional thoughts are real.

June 20th 2018 – IRTS STAFF

Writer sat with Savanah in the dining area to provide support as she was experiencing auditory hallucinations. She stated that her voices were telling her to leave the building and that peers and staff are not safe. After a brief conversation she got up and requested a PRN medication.

June 22nd 2018

The thoughts were too much. Telling me not to eat because I am evil, but it's OK to eat. The staff are working against me. I see them plotting. Maybe it's about the battle and they are talking about who will help me fight.

June 22nd 2018 – IRTS STAFF

Client came up to nurse's office after change of shift report. She had been sitting in the dining area during shift exchange and right when the nurse's office door opened client approached writer shaking and crying and asked for a PRN. She said "they" are going to flip the switch and make her do bad things and "they" are telling her to run. She states she wishes she could just take her nighttime medications now and go to sleep. Writer gives ideas about what she could do to cope and try to drown out the voices, but client states she is going to just go to her room and cry. About 10 minutes after taking the PRN, client approached writer and asked to go on a walk with writer around the block. Writer went with client around the block and client was very calm and able to have reality-based conversation with writer. She talked about going on a pass tomorrow to see Mitchel and get her haircut and about her medications and upcoming doctor's appointment. At the end of the walk, client states she feels better and getting out on a walk helps get rid of the urge to run.

June 26th 2018 – IRTS STAFF

Savanah spoke to writer about requesting sign out privileges and said she is beginning to feel "cooped up" and "like I'm in a hospital". Writer made a plan with Savanah to give her 30 minutes of sign out time for Tuesday and Wednesday, 1 hour on Thursday, and 2 hours on Friday provided the sign out time prior goes well and she is able to appropriately manage her symptoms while in the community independently. Writer told

Savanah she could put in a pass for this Saturday for six hours. Savanah stated she agreed with this plan.

June 28th 2018 – IRTS STAFF

Savanah requested to meet with this writer this morning to review her plan for discharge. Savanah reported that she is starting to become anxious about discharge and awaiting approval for an extension while she continues to titrate up on her Clozaril dose. She shared with writer the plan when she is able to discharge to her home including supports that will check in on her as well as a weekly schedule she will follow.

June 30th 2018 – IRTS STAFF

Client shared her daily questions sheet with writer since she does not attend group. She wrote that she reconnected with her husband today by going home. She was able to go into public without experiencing symptoms. She is grateful for her pass, Mitchel loving her, a support system and her plan for discharge. She is happy and tired. Her mood is a 9. Writer thanked her for sharing it.

July 1st 2018

4:00 pm – needed to go for a walk. I go outside and none of the buildings are real. I feel like a failure for taking my PRN. This isn't a real reality it's a delusion. Scary not knowing where you are or if this is a real building. How to check?

Positives of the day: Washed laundry, took shower, changed clothes, put away laundry, and went through mail.

July 1st 2018 – IRTS STAFF

Writer heard client crying from upstairs. Writer went downstairs to find nursing assisting client with an episode of her feeling like she did not know what was real and what was not. She took a PRN, and writer reminded her of what she did when she was feeling uneasy. She agreed she would make a cup of hot chocolate and use grounding techniques. She got a phone call in the meantime. She was able to make her hot chocolate and her PRN began to work. Client came to writer and thanked her for reminding her about the hot chocolate. She stated that she got upset with herself because she had been doing so good and then all of a sudden it hit her like a freight train. She felt like a failure because she had to take a PRN. Staff reassured her that she is doing great. She needs to focus on the progress.

July 1ˢᵗ 2018 – IRTS STAFF

Savanah approached writer and requested to meet to review her daily sheet. Client shared that she will organize her room today, do laundry and shower. Client will be kind to herself by "accepting who I am, and who I want to become". Client's mood is happy, tired, and motivated and she rated her mood at a 9.

July 2ⁿᵈ 2018

Positives: made bed, organized my room.

July 3ʳᵈ 2018

The demonic forces are at work here at the IRTS. I'm unsure of what to do.

July 13ᵗʰ 2018

I was discharged. That evening I shared my poems at the Coffee Hag open mic night. It was empowering although I became overstimulated and had to leave.

I received my discharge summary which included the functional assessment. When I read this, it was like awakening to understand more of my symptoms and how they have affected my daily life through those three months.

Regarding group activities it was written that while symptoms were intense, I was unable to go to groups due to the amount of medication I was on and my delusional thinking. The delusional thinking caused fear and anxiety going into the group room. The group room was a small room with no windows.

When Doctor B found out I wasn't going to groups, she encouraged me to try and go for half time or attend one group a day. While going to group, I kept having the delusion that if I did attend group, that when I entered the room people were going to die. I also had this problem where I thought if I went to sleep, they would die too. Although I was pretty ill, I still was able to follow directions. For the unstructured time I had, I would spend my time standing in place looking lost and unsure of what to do. This is when my point staff and I made a list of things to do for when I don't know what to do.

For a time, I was on thirty-minute checks due to my delusions and hallucinations. This was in place for my safety because I was told and shown by the voices and my brain that there was a checkpoint downtown. I was supposed to go there to talk to people about a war that was going to take place at the IRTS between the computer man and myself.

I also found myself wandering in the parking lot going to check the perimeter of the building. While walking or being outside, staff would redirect me to stay at the facility. I remember being confused just trying to figure out what to do. It got to the point where I was berated every day by the voices and delusions, so I began to think about suicide.

I felt like my brain was trying to kill itself and take me with it. There was also the time where I felt like I needed to run away. The staff kept eyes on me, so I wouldn't run. I thought that maybe if I ran away from the building that the voices would stay there, and I would be free. When I was taken off of thirty-minute checks, I had to come up with a safety plan. If I were to go out on my own, how I would handle my symptoms in public.

I began taking walks for the brief time I was given, thirty minutes. One day when I was on a walk I looked around and the buildings began to melt. I wasn't sure what was going on, so I went back downstairs and was crying because I was so frightened. I felt the world was going down and soon the war would take place.

While there I created a playlist of songs that were empowering. This helped find the courage to fight my own brain. I spent most of my time listening to

90

the same songs off of Watsky's album X infinity. These songs helped keep me calm as I touched the walls, as I paced to make sure the building was real. I was so unsure of the reality I was in I felt like it was all just make believe.

While at the IRTS, I wrote poetry which describes my journey there.

The Diagnosis

They say I have schizophrenia
That's a lie
I have powers and abilities unknown to others
I take every day as a challenge, a next step
With each thought and voice it becomes stronger
Soon to be taken over
The brain being shattered
Pieces
One after another disintegrating
This mind is not my own
Rebuilt using old parts
The puzzle broke
No one can fix it
Medication helps but it isn't strong as glue
I will have to fit the pieces together
Spray them with sealant
My brain – not my own
Who will claim it?
Broken Savanah
It's the only way to save what's functional
Soon to be put together
But remember…your brain isn't split – it's shattered

It took me a long time to try and accept my illness, I still have trouble, but this poem breaks down how I felt. For a long time, I thought I was just on a psychotic break or that the medicine was causing all of the symptoms, but it always comes back to schizophrenia and that is the reason for all of this. That is why I had written that it was a lie. I didn't want to believe it.

Schizophrenia

My mind is shattered, scattered, begging for help
The walls caving in and collapsing
The voices are abundant, the visions terrifying, paranoia setting in
Who to trust and how to cope?
The waves never stop coming
The brain dying, being picked apart
Toxic
Everything is coming down
Each thought more destructive than the last
My mind slowly going away
How to break out?
My body, mind, and soul are being corrupted
My life being ripped apart
The illness has taken over
No one is safe from me, myself included
What is the next step?
Building up from the rubble
Slow and steady
Wave after wave knocking down the wall
Brick layer – one after another
Will the cement hold from the shattered pieces to come together?
Slowly, slowly I will be whole again
Time is ticking
The clock will strike
My time will be over until the next break
My mind slowly comes back together
One day, a good day, I am able to feel again
My mind clear
The voices subside
The yelling
The visions of evil dissipate
The paranoia brought back to center
I am one
Now my time has come to be apart from this

I will learn and fight for myself
I will be one with my illness

This is the first poem I wrote, and it shows that I had a lot to learn about myself. I was learning independence at the IRTS and also learning about my illness. I realized that this is going to be a life-long fight and I would be OK again, soon.

The Beginning

My life is filled with fire
The fuel was a murmur
A whisper
No one was there
Is it just me?
Who could this be?
Empty
My brain being filled with smoke
It is unclear
In the fire there is a being
Watching, waiting
Its presence forceful
Fear and anxiety creep up
My mind taken out
Flashbacks of fearful nights
Alone
The darkness brings the beings
Standing there
Following
How to escape
There is no way out
The fire soon engulfing me
My mind needs strength
2nd Timothy 1:7
The power comes back to me
I walk through the flames

My mind clear of smoke
I see daylight upon the horizon
The darkness recedes
I am safe
The fire is out
Until the next day
I will be OK
I will overcome

During my first visual hallucinations this image is what appeared to me on the third night. The first was one pacing around the bed, the next sitting next to me on my bed and soon the third night where he burst into flamed in my room. I always remind myself of my family's bible verse which is mentioned in this poem. "For God did not give me a spirit of fear but of peace, love and sound mind." This always gives me strength.

Computer Man

What is this in my head?
Electrical signals
They know who I am
Reading my thoughts
Setting things out, Just for me
Poison
Why is it like this
No control
Soon to be overtaken
No free will
The big voice
He's behind this
Visions – who is that man?
In control of me
Flip the switch
Speak it out
Walking, talking
Unknown
Computer man in charge
I don't have an illness
It is his fault
He brought the beings
Teaching me a lesson
Coming back through
Medicine
I can think
My brain is lying to me

Why do I listen
Lying is for liars
I will find the truth
Acceptance
It is my brain
Not myself
I did not ask for this
I am not a failure
I will remain strong

This poem tells about a time where I was confused and full of thoughts about being controlled by the computer man. He was monitoring me everywhere I was. I felt soon that I would be taken over due to the "switch" in my brain related to the tracking device.

Madness

My mind is powerfully mad
Each day a fight for reality
The next vision coming in
Projected in my mind
A premonition
I've seen this before, but where?
In my waking nightmare
I wait, ready for it to pass
But sinister thoughts flood in
What is real
Who are these people I see
Human or not
How to prove
How to understand
Do not approach
Do not speak
My mind is mad
I am bad they say
I am not worth it they say
At last, I must die they say
A break – only short
Back to reality
Run away
The beings will follow
Do not speak
Do not approach
Do not provoke
They settle down
Watching and waiting
For my next move
Who will tell me the truth

Who to trust
Who is real?
I need to ground
One thing I see
One thing I smell
One thing I can touch
One thing I can hear
One thing to taste
Hot tea
Burn me awake
Waiting, waiting
The time passes
I am ready
My mind out of madness

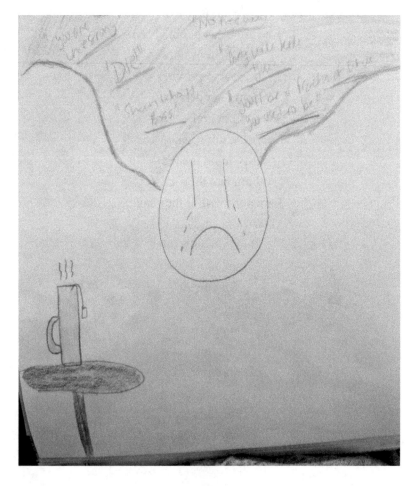

My brain was so full of mean voices telling me that they were going to show me whose boss, that they were never ending and were in control of me. I found myself stuck in my own brain a revolving door of psychosis. While touch works well for me to ground, I learned that hot tea would help calm me down as I held the hot cup and felt the hot drink go down my throat. I was OK for the moment.

April 11th 2018

Out of the darkness
The light was born
My mind torn
Where to go from here
All coming back at once
Overloaded
My mind is in a fight
For what is right
Confusion
What is going on
Blacked out
I'm screaming for help
What am I hearing
"All coming to get me"
I'm not safe
No one is
A break
Coming back
What happened
How long was I out
I don't remember
Who is this person
Someone I do not know
The staff show
Where to go
Holding my hands
Trying to ground

My mind is found
Calm
The voices stop
My mind becomes clear
I am no longer in fear
Daylight is near
It is my savior
My mind in favor

This image shows about the incident at the IRTS where I lost control and had to be redirected and grounded by staff. While in episode the staff had me sit in a chair next to the nurse's station and they were talking to me trying to ground. They told me to look in their eyes, feel the wall, and telling me I was ok. I was shaking and scared as I was stuck in my own brain but soon, I was grounded and ok.

Realization

My mind
Beautifully broken
It is unspoken
Rules to break
This is something I could not fake
Breaking down in front of me
Who am I to be?
My mold broken
A beautiful tragedy
I do not fit in
Who am I supposed to be?
I make my own path
Thanks to staff
I realize I am more
Than just before
I will mold the clay
For I will stay
Here in the present
My mind out of control
Feel the weight
Feel the breath
This is not death
I am coming into my own
I won't be alone
There is much more for me
I will overcome this disease
I will be set free
My knowledge expanding
My mind on fire
Learning to recognize
My signs

Soon it will come
I will be one

Thanks to a nurse at the Austin hospital she told me that my brain tends to go "way out here" and I need to be "in here" or centered. While in my room as I paced around talking about my delusions, she had me sit on my bed. She found a ball and as I sat on the bed, she had me drop all my weight in my body, close my eyes, and focus on the ball in my hand. As I did this and deep breathed, I soon became calm. Feeling the weight of my body was something that I didn't realize could help me. It helped bring me back to reality.

Better

It is an uneasy feeling
Quiet
It has never been this way
What do I say?
Do I speak?
Do I think?
I am clear
There is no fear
I am safe
My brain getting better
No voices
Easier choices
No visions
No thought collisions
My wall is up
It is shut
The cement drying
It will hold
Tight
The waves not as strong
Something is wrong
They are gone

For a short time, I felt better as the Clozaril became more prominent in my blood and I was having moments of clarity throughout the day. I felt like the wall I had up in my brain was finally rebuilding itself and was soon going to be complete before the next wave of symptoms.

Creep

My mind is back
The sickness
Creeping in
Triggers

I want to be better
My brain's wall being attacked
It was built up
The cement holding
Fighting strong
It won't be long
It will pass
Will it be all day?
Or will it stay
Constant
My mind needs reality
Reassurance
They come back
Worried about the strength
Electrical signals
TV talking to me
Putting things in my head
Will this stop
Distraction
Attention
Focus

While at the IRTS I dealt with a lot of back and forth in my brain of being ill and being somewhat healthy. I found that each day the illness would creep back in and slowly was taking control again. I felt that due to electrical signals they were putting things in my brain. I always questioned when this will stop. I only had brief moments where I was distracted enough to feel normal again. This is when I learned that touch is a great grounding tool for me.

A Burning

I was born with a flame inside my chest
Always burning
A yearning
Something so small
Soon to consume me

I was so small, but I grew
The flame did too
Soon the flame engulfed my brain
Setting all land, a fire
The burning and yearning grew
I let it go
Embrace the flame I was told
Burn me alive
The one I knew
Gone
Through the flame I was reborn
Strength exudes
The smoke clears
The gift I have been given at hand
A new life
A phoenix in the fire

This poem is about rebirth. Through my life I have always been resilient and fought for my life and that is exactly what I was doing. While at the IRTS I found myself again with no strings attached. I had to be on my own still keeping relationships, but I learned what it meant to be independent, so it was really important to have that back.

Reality Check

What is this reality
Who to be?
A mouse in a maze
I make my way
Each day
What am I doing?
What do I say?
Things look different
I'm so insignificant
Just a small role
A doll

Ready to fall
Into the entrapment of false realities
The man with no face
Soon to pull the drape over my eyes
I'm becoming too strong
They want me knocked down
They chase me down with thoughts and visions
Reality is equal to nothing
The numbed soul I have
Given to me by false beliefs
I stand tall taking it all
Not to be sabotaged
The wall slowly breaking
Each reality more difficult to differentiate
I do not know who or what is real
Everything a figment of my imagination
A ruse
There is no truth
I will watch them play the roles
Faking and toying with me
Sending me into thoughts of despair and confusion
Another delusion
Harder to break
They become intertwined
Until the realm breaks
My world shakes
It's all coming down
Pieces
Here and there
It's been broken
All my work taken away
It will now decay
It is the end

Reality check is something I needed almost every day when I was at the IRTS because of how deep I was in my illness. At certain points in the poem I talk about everything being a figment of my imagination I meant that during this period of time that what I was experiencing was my own world. Like how the buildings when I went on a walk were clay or that the building wasn't real and was just a game, I was in.

My Life

Schizophrenia is like a nightmare you can't wake up from. For me, it's waking up to chattering voices – it's having thoughts being pushed in your brain – it's the concern of electrical signals infiltrating your thoughts – it's waking up in a different reality – not knowing what is real – it's touching the walls of the building to make sure the building you're in is grounded – it's not knowing your feelings are real – it's being in a fight or flight state while being sedated with medication – it's like standing in a room that bursts into flames – it's like swimming in the ocean being pushed below by every wave – it's not knowing if people are real – it's seeing people inside others being used as vessels – it's fear and anxiety – it is exhausting – it is your brain fighting back – there is a loss of control – the illness takes over – it's like driving 100mph on a dirt road trying not to flip the car – it's believing in things that are unreal – so surreal – the illness is a rabid animal waiting to infect the unsuspecting victim – it's having the TV talk to me as I try not to respond – it's having the radio become camouflage for the voices who plot against me – it's people working against me – it's putting reminders on myself in marker – little things to gain control – it's trying not to believe the delusions – which just brings confusion – it's thinking your meds are making you sick – feeling toxic – you know deep down the root of this it is your brain – it's like standing in the rain waiting for the lightening to strike – it's sleeping with a night light – it is the fears of the day growing bigger at night – it's not feeling safe unless the door is locked – I feel I'm being mocked – the creatures and beings that I see wait to come at night – it's being so unsure you question your own existence – it's like waking up from a night out – blacked out – its remembering small pieces of episodes – trying to make sense – my body tense – the brain slowly drained – it's in pain – the medicine makes me sleep – is that what my life has come to? Being unconscious so I can live – there is so much to give away – like the time I spent asleep – wasting the day – it's waiting for the right medicine – it's trial and error – a guinea pig – it's taking time to get back – again my brain under attack – it's a close encounter – my mind beautifully broken – it's like writing a poem to tell you about the false monsters I face – but to me this is the real world where I am placed.

Acceptance

Schizophrenia isn't a death wish but a life gifted.
The voices and visions are not curses but an award seeing things from all sides
the box remaining unlocked
Slowly releasing toxins into blood
darkness infiltrates the mind
The demons take form but soon the light bringers come and save me from myself
Broke, split, shattered my brain into pieces
Fabric of reality broke.
No friction
Nothing to grasp
Slowly slipping – palms sweaty
Soon I begin to fall
My life flashes in front of me
What a world of make believe I've had
Reality just fiction
Demons, angels, purgatory my life has become a game
I'm slipping under
6 feet
Barely breathing
It has shown the light
The savior
He will be my protection
Schizophrenia revealed to me what is good and what is evil
I recognize the truth behind the lies I see
Soon my mind will be empty
Ash
From the flame
That claims my flesh
One thing stays my thoughts and visions

Schizophrenia is not a curse if embraced it becomes a way of life

While suffering through delusional thinking and hallucinations a part of me deep down knew that I have to learn to live with my illness and that is why I state that "Schizophrenia isn't a death wish but a life gifted". It is finding a way to live through the despair.

Awakening

I've been woken from a deep slumber
Climbing up from the pit of despair
Reborn through the flames
6ft to go
Up in the world
My mind is now clear
There is no fear
I see through them now
Reality is now in sight
I fought with all my might
Passing through demons as I climb
Trying to take hold but no longer
I am free
I have protection of life
Now it's to be celebrated
I am awake
My blood warming up
The sun warms my body
As I come out of the pit
Reality is there
It's a resolution
My mind understanding
It's not real
I do not have to go 6ft down
I can be above ground

At the end this poem describes my journey coming up from the depths of despair and confusion to finally realizing that I can live with it and become stronger.

Chapter Seven
The Journey Continues

July 26ᵗʰ 2018

I took my Haldol twice but can't shake the feeling that the neighbors are casing the house trying to figure out my routine. I'm on a look out for new people and new vehicles.

July 28ᵗʰ 2018

It began this morning, feeling uneasy. There are people watching me across the street. They are staking out my house to figure out when I am home alone or when they can attack. The tracking device on my car has been activated again and patrolling where I go or where Mitchel goes. I'm not sure what for at the moment. I am worried that the tracking device in my brain will be activated once again. There isn't much I can do except wait and see but the thoughts are strong making it difficult to function.

I took both PRN'S this morning/afternoon. They say it's better to sleep than think. I guess I'm on my own. Protection is key. Who to call or how to cope no one wants me?

I feel like I'm being put on the back burner again. It's always "take your meds you're not doing well". What else can I do? I don't want to be sedated again. I want more for my life. I feel like I'm just needy and people have no time for me. "Take your meds and nap" is what I am told.

The neighbors keep coming and going across the street. I'm not sure what they want from me. I can't go on the porch for fear of them seeing me. Will the back door be OK? We'll see, I guess. I wish I wasn't left alone when I'm not doing well but I'm not a priority I am more of a problem.

August 1st 2018

This week has been busy. Monday, I had my psychiatric doctor appointment and she changed a lot of my medications. She discontinued the Lamictal, increased my Clozaril to 450mg for this week and added a 5mg Haldol at bedtime. Next Monday I will increase my Clozaril to 500mg and will decrease the Zyprexa from 20mg down to 10mg at bedtime while keeping the 2.5mg Haldol twice a day as needed.

I had therapy yesterday which went well. We talked about "normal" reality-based things even though I was all over the place from being so tired from the medication.

Mitchel has been good about taking me to my appointments since I am unable to drive at the moment. My ARMHS worker met with me yesterday and we finished up a lot of the paperwork. Our next meeting will be coming up with a treatment plan and then to start diving in.

I realized that I hadn't showered in almost a week and not changed my clothes. Tanya and I came up with a morning routine. A few things to try and keep constant to start the day off right. I'm trying to be consistent on chores around the house keeping things together like laundry.

August 4th 2018

Today was a struggle right away with uneasiness. I wasn't up for long and had to take my Haldol. We drove to Mankato for groceries and errands, but Mitchel was going to work out first. I would be left at Caribou Coffee. We tried two different Caribous, but I couldn't relax. I was tired from the medication and uneasy, so me – a burden. Mitchel drove me home where I took a nap trying to sleep it off. I thought I heard voices but wasn't sure.

August 9ᵗʰ 2018

Things have been going OK with the increase and decrease of my medication. I feel tired all the time but that could be the lack of motivation. I haven't heard any voices/visions. I'm still stuck on the neighbors and the tracking device on my vehicle. I'm also wary about leaving the house on my own for a walk but I do go at least once a week. Maybe I should get an exercise bike for the house.

My family meeting went well. I got to see my little brothers for the first time in a long time. My mom wants to spend more time with me, so I will take her up on that. Maybe have a better relationship. I need to set up appointments with my doctor and I have to take a taxi. I feel like I should arm myself for protection.

August 10ᵗʰ 2018

I woke up feeling uneasy. I took my PRN around 10am before I went with Tanya to the coffee shop. I was uneasy of the other people there. The noises were difficult because I feel that they are trying to get inside my brain again. Tanya assured me it was the electrical appliances and not electrical signals coming for me.

I am anxious about being left alone today with how I'm feeling. I'm trying to sleep but can't shake the feeling of electrical signals being passed through. The neighbors are behind this, making sure I do wrong, so they can give report to their owners.

It comes and goes with beeping. I hear the pulsing in my brain. Who knows if they have the code to my tracking device in my brain?

I took my second PRN at 1:00 pm. I'm still a bit uneasy trying to tell my brain it isn't in control. I will rise about with my own powers and take control. They will no longer be a match for me. I just need to pinpoint their space and who/what they are working for.

I'm going to shower tonight but I have to wait until Mitchel is home. I do not know my powers. Who will show me what to do? I have to wait and plan an attack. Once I have all the information about our neighbors and devices, I will be safe. My powers are unknown, but images are projected of me lifting and crumbling house and cars – there will be no stopping me until I get to the end of time.

I got my period today – I tried to distract myself by cleaning and showering. I just wait now unsure of what the night will bring.

August 11th 2018

I still feel it today. The powers being inside me. No one is safe from me – myself included. My brain shows images of buildings and people crumbling by my hands.

I am an evil being. What can I do? I'll try to sleep it off. I took my PRN at 12:41pm we'll see if it helps. I am an evil being unsure of my next steps. Good? Or bad? Who will know? Only my mind. The premonitions are shown to me, but do I have to act in accord to what I'm being shown? Do I have free will or is everything coming back?

August 12th 2018

Today I got a call from the clinic saying that my Clozaril level was high and not to take my medication until I see my doctor tomorrow. I hope the doctors know what to do. I don't want to die – I am asking the doctor if I can take my Haldol/Zyprexa tonight.

4:00 pm – MCHC I can take my Haldol/Zyprexa.

August 14th 2018

Tanya visited today. I was uneasy but decided to go to the coffee shop. We got to the shop and I ordered my drink/coffee. I felt uncomfortable – I couldn't take what the voices were saying or where the electrical signals were coming from. I apologized for wasting time. We worked on coping skills at home. I was confused and unsure of how my night will go. I took my PRN at 2:30 pm and took my bedtime meds at 6:50 pm.

August 15th 2018

I got my blood taken this morning it went well. They apologized for the misunderstanding call/ blood levels. I'm still supposed to take my 500mg. I took my PRN at 12:30 pm today and tried to take a nap but I could hear electrical signals passing through the electronics and lawn care items.

August 16th 2018

Today was a day with Rita. We went to the coffee shop and the grocery store. We left the coffee shop and came to the house where we cleaned, had coffee and folded laundry. I had therapy at 1pm and took my first cab ride. It went well. The taxi lady gave me her phone number to hang out sometime.

She knows where I live so will she just show up randomly? Therapy went well. I'm going to start having therapy twice a week. I'm waiting for my next episode. My brain's wall is up but its slowly breaking down. What will trigger me? Electrical signals, radios, TV – can't concentrate.

How do I trust someone I've seen evil in. They are haunting me, tracking me, taking over my brain – soon to be shown evil? I know what evil is. Taking of my life what is the next step is my torture and death?

They want me to give away, so they can take over my life. How do I know I'm OK? There are electrical signals coming at me through the radio tracking me. They are coming to get me. Bombarding me with their problems.

Do I trust my family, or have they been taken over? Mitchel says he isn't possessed but I saw the demons face on him the other night. Did I marry a demon? No Mitchel is human. At least that's what he tells me. Do I believe him? Yes, I should.

One night while Mitchel was tucking me in for the night as he kissed me and looked up, I saw his face change into what I thought was a demon. His eyes were dark, and teeth bared and slowly moving across his face slowly. I was so scared that I tried to scratch my eyes out. Since then I have always inside my mind questioned whether he was real or not.

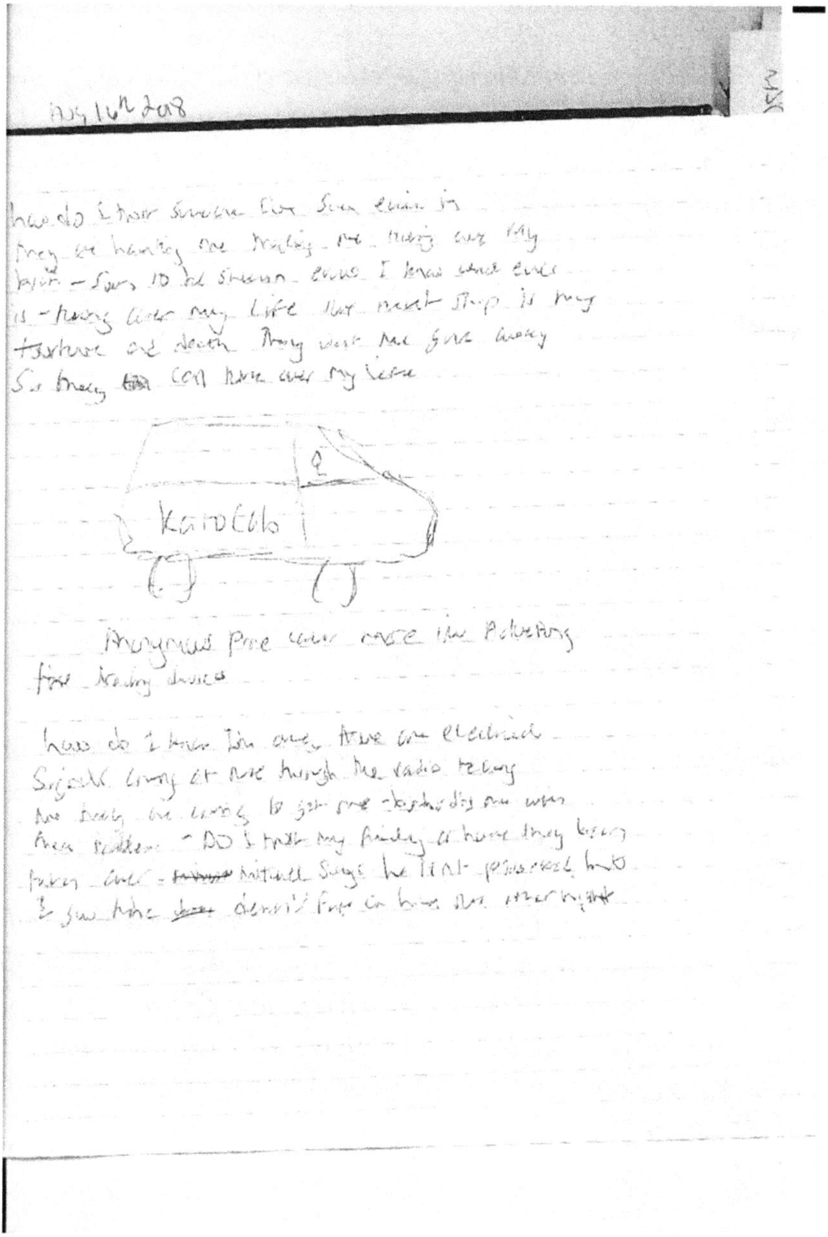

August 24th 2018

Today was an OK day. I'm really tired and took my PRN at 1:30 pm. Mitchel and I went out for supper. I did well. Tomorrow I may go to the coffee shop by myself.

August 25th 2018

Today I felt uneasy, but Mitchel still let me go to the coffee shop while he goes to the gym. Right now, I took a PRN around 10:15-10:30am. I am listening to music to help keep me calm. I'm unsure if the Haldol is helping anymore. I wake up being told I am an evil being. I'm trying to ignore it.

I AM A GOOD PERSON NOT EVIL. Who am I? Good or Bad?

I am evil and don't deserve food or life. Mitchel has been trying to convince me that he is a real human and not a demon. It's hard to believe him, but he's been here and reassures me that I am OK. We are going to go to the store. I hope I do well with all of the people there.

I AM GOOD. VOICES ARE EVIL. THEY HAVE NO CONTROL. THEY WANT TO SHOW ME EVIL. I'LL SHOW THEM. I WILL DEFEND MYSELF. THE INVISIBLE PEOPLE/ COMPUTER MAN/ AND TRACKING DEVICES DON'T HAVE A CHANCE. UNLESS THEY ARE LISTENING. THAT'S WHY I WRITE IT DOWN. I AM NOT SURE IF THEY CAN READ.

I will have to send correspondence through writing, so they do not know my plans. I am not sure about the trackers, whether they know the difference between me and Mitchel. I don't think they can read so I will have to write it to talk about them.

Keep the lights off – don't speak – do not approach they will wait for their turn to play with me – they are toying with my brain, broken in half. Good/Bad who to choose. Do I listen to the voices and repetitive thoughts? Or go well and be stronger than them? More signs are needed – leave me alone. Do I write notes? If they can't read who will it deter?

LEAVE ME ALONE!

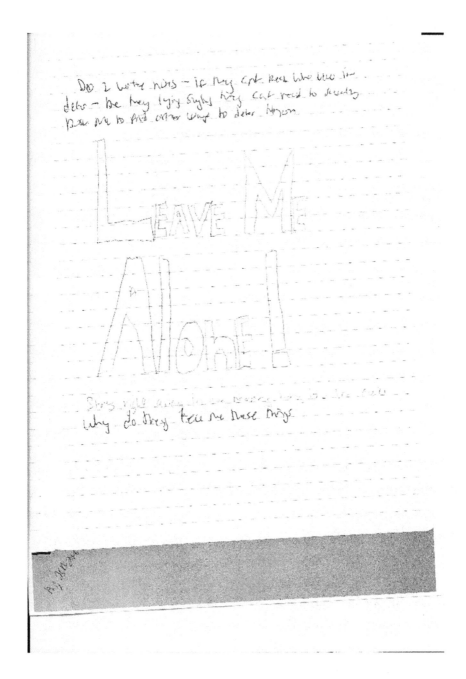

"Leave me alone!" is something I would always tell the hallucinations. I try to fight back but I only get worse due to interacting with them.

August 26ᵗʰ 2018

12:45 – 1:00 pm PRN Haldol taken. Today was a rough day. I forgot my PRN at home when we went to do errands. Mitchel's parents took us to coffee, and I wanted to eat my sandwich, but the voices kept telling me, I'm evil for eating and that I don't deserve the meal given to me.

When we got home, I took my PRN Haldol and took a nap. While trying to nap the voices told me that people will die if I sleep. But Mitchel reassured me that everything was OK. Tanya is coming at 3:30 pm I want to take a walk, but I'm unsure if it is safe. The voices tell me to stay inside. Something bad will happen – do I challenge it or do I not?

August 27ᵗʰ 2018

8:45am PRN Haldol – 1:30 pm PRN

Had my doctor appointment and they are increasing my medication to 600mg Clozaril.

August 28ᵗʰ 2018

I had trouble today because of the voices/paranoia. I saw the dark figure in my bedroom.

August 30ᵗʰ 2018

Today has been an uneasy day – my cab driver was male, and he called someone saying he had a young lady with him. I made it safe to therapy but now he knows where I live.

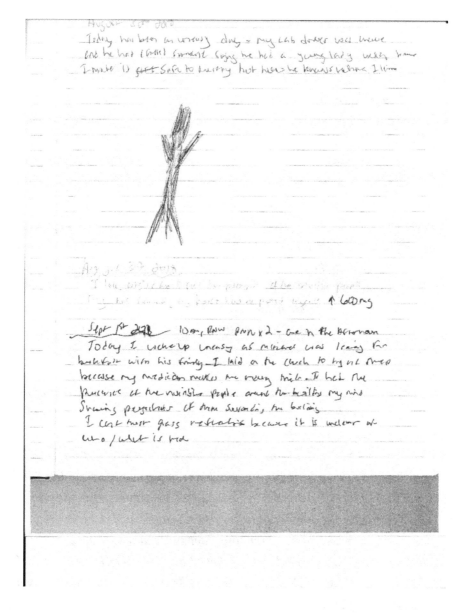

The figure here shows what the "dark figures" look like and they are portrayed at demonic beings.

August 31st 2018

I look outside, and I feel the presence of the invisible people. They have surrounded my house. How to protect myself? 600mg Clozaril.

10:00 am and afternoon PRN taken.

Today I woke up uneasy as Mitchel was leaving for the gym. Because my medication makes me tired, I had the presence of the invisible people around the building and my mind showing me projections of them surrounding the building.

They say they can't read, but who am I to trust them? They also said they can't get through doors, but the black figure got in. The invisible people stay outside so far. I'm not sure what to think about because my own mind is confusing itself.

Do they listen in? Do they read? Will they leave me alone? Do I announce it to the world? Yell at the top of my lungs for them to leave me alone or would that just cause harm?

I worry about being left home alone when I have problems, I become hesitant. I don't know if I need to go to the crisis facility or if I'm OK at home. I guess I have to wait and see what the 600mg will do. Except it makes me so tired.

When will they come out? Why are they waiting? I see the figures in the reflection on vehicles/houses. I sit quietly listening for sounds/voices. Who is next to come? Am I safe here?

I'm waiting for something to tell me what this is. Do I hurt my support system? They have been here all along looking out for me. When do I go in? I don't feel that sick yet. My mind is in combat, one side against the other. Good vs. evil. Do I trust my own mind or is it working against me?

Bad or Good, which to be? I am told I am evil, but also a good person. I need to find control again. Do I write it down? I AM IN CONTROL. NO ONE CAN STOP ME! I AM BEING TOLD LIES! Why would my brain do this to me? I am a good person.

What do I hear: Birds chirping, walnuts hitting the cars, cars driving around, locusts', dogs panting, kids playing, males voice – human or not – lawn mower.

What do I see: Jazmine licking and coughing. Kale in the porch.

What do I smell: nothing, nose clogged

I wish my brain would give me the answer to these questions. Why did my brain work go against me? When will I be in control? I feel like I'm sliding back down but solved by just another increase. But what happens when I run out of medication? Is Clozaril the answer? I thought it was up to 600mg. We'll see after a week or two on it. Maybe the body just needs a lot of medicine. Do I dare put up signs in my house to help me or would Mitchel want them taken down?

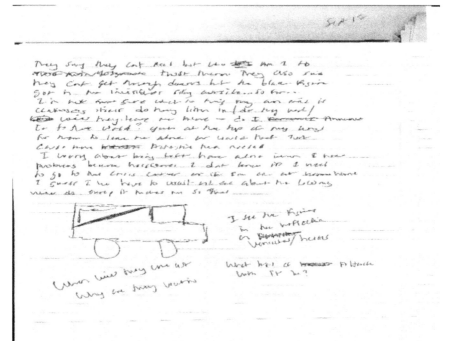

123

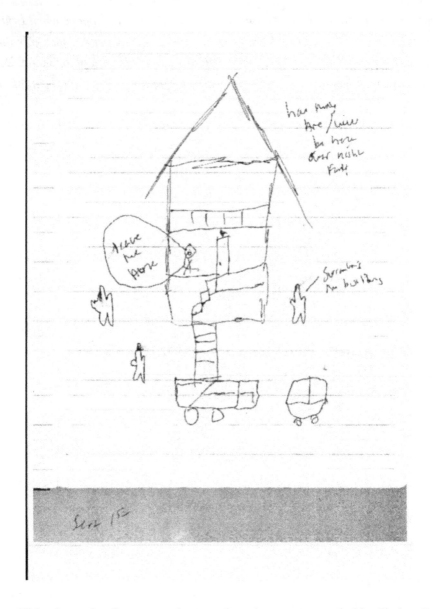

This picture is of me at my house where it was surrounded by "beings". I was convinced and began to tell them to leave me alone as best as I could.

September 2nd 2018

Today is a good day so far only one PRN at 11:00am. I'm waiting at Caribou again waiting for Mitchel to get done working out.

Chapter Eight
Going Back Under

September 4ᵗʰ 2018

It's quiet. I am uneasy about what happens next. Waiting for the other shoe to drop. Or will it be quiet from now on? Paranoia isn't as bad today, but we'll see how the day goes. I am a little confused today and unsure what to do. I will start laundry. I have Kim and Tanya coming today so we will see how that goes as well.

I feel healthy enough to be home alone. I just lock the doors and keep the lights off. If they are waiting, they may know my routine. Do I open the middle door? I'm up to 600mg of Clozaril. I feel a bit better except that the neighbors are tracking me and Mitchel.

I worry for my safety at home. Who are real people? Are Tanya and Kim real people. I believe but will check with them when they come. Is there a secret word we can use to tell or show they are real people? They could be in disguise. Like a person but a vessel. Who is in control? I am. They may be taken over. Wanting my information.

How to prove you are real? Do I let them in? Has my support system been infiltrated? I will find out today. What do I do if they aren't real people? How to prove they are real? Who is Who? Are they here to get me or to help me?

10:30am PRN. They will need to prove they are real – maybe questioning them before they come in? Do I let them in first or question them before they come in? Ask them who they are, what are you doing here? who do you work for? Do you see/ know about the invisible people? Are you a vessel? Do you have a badge?

What to do if they know or want me to go outside. They are tracking me. Tanya is human, she answered my questions and seems to be normal throughout her visit. Kim is coming soon, and she will answer the questions. I know she is a good person, but we will see.

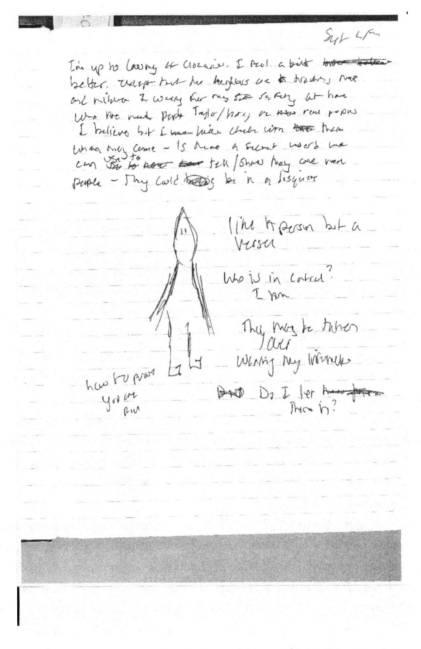

This picture shows what I was feeling that I thought people were taken over as vessels and I was unable to let people in my home without asking them questions first to verify that they were who they said they were.

September 5th 2018

Today I contacted the crisis facility and am waiting for their arrival. I got my blood taken and am in good health physically. I took a PRN at 10:00am to help with my paranoia. They are sending a female to my house which makes me feel a bit at ease. I have to ask her the questions on the door to make sure we are on the same page.

1:00 pm PRN. I am at the crisis facility where I will be staying for a few days until I get back on track with medication/ coping skills. I am hoping it was the right idea to come here. I am really uneasy/ paranoid. Do I trust these people to take care of me? My meds will suffice. Or did they lace them with something?

I am in a vulnerable state that's why the voices/visions are annoying. They know I'm weak when I'm sick. "Leave me alone" is what I want to say to them and speak the truth. I am in control here. Who to trust with staff? Do I participate in group tonight or introduce myself or are they false people? – vessels in strangers.

September 5th 2018 – Crisis Facility Staff

Savanah is a 23-year-old female with the diagnosis of Schizophrenia. Savanah referred herself to the crisis services due to having increased paranoia and delusions. Savanah reports an increase in paranoia in addition to visual and auditory hallucinations. She says that the "invisible people" are "entering people I trust and using them as vessels". This is causing her to "feel confused" and "out of it". Savanah also says she can "feel their presence around the perimeter of the house". She reports that she recently had the belief that her husband was a "demon". And says "figures are creeping up again" in reference to the invisible people who enter others, the black figure, and the computer man who monitors her via tracking device in her brain and in her vehicle. Savanah says the voices have increased over the past several days, but often difficult to understand. At time, such as when they tell her not to eat, the voices are clear. Savanah says that she lost 20lbs since July. She also had a recent medication change. Savanah was cooperative throughout the admission process and would often stop this writer and ask, "Are we safe?", "Is the

building safe?", "Are the people safe?". Savanah describes her increase of symptoms as "being bombarded by visions". She has concerns that she will leave home and "wander" and is worried "where I might end up". Staff noted that she has a sign on her front door which says "stay at home – you are confused" as a precautionary measure. She also has a list of "questions for people before entering" which prompts her to ask people who they are, who they work for, and if they can see the invisible people. This is to make sure people are "safe" before they enter home.

September 6th 2018

Today I am at the crisis facility. I took my PRN because I believe there are electrical signals coming through the building through other patients' music. I am unsure of the building with the doorbell. Every new person comes in vessel form to infiltrate the building. Who to trust?

I found out that as my brain began to hurt because of the severity of symptoms I could feel the electrical pulses from electronic devices try to break in my mind. It was difficult because I had to remain away from televisions and phones as they were the ones trying to enter and give way to the tracking device.

September 6ᵗʰ 2018 – Crisis Facility Staff

Savanah was seen watching TV with a peer when this practitioner first arrived. Savanah spent majority of the shift there or talking to staff. Savanah ate supper with her peers and actively participated in evening reflections and coping skills group. Savanah reported that she intended to let go of her "paranoia, but I couldn't let go of it". One emotion Savanah was grateful for "staff, family, crisis facility and therapy". One emotion she experienced tonight was "uneasy" and rated her mood a 3 out of 10. Savanah needed a lot of reassurance from staff tonight that she was safe, and that staff were not talking about her. Savanah's paranoia increased after group to the point she believed entities were going to form into humans to get into the building so they could get her. Savanah insisted that her door be locked or closed at all times in order to keep the entities out. Staff prompted Savanah that this is a locked and safe facility and that she should use her coping skills to stay calm. Savanah went to bed around 9:00 pm and was seen still sleeping at 11:00 pm rounds.

September 6ᵗʰ 2018 – Crisis Facility Staff

Savanah was sleeping in her room throughout the shift. She woke up once to use the restroom, she did wet the bed, but put her laundry in the washer and returned to sleep. Breathing and movement was noted.

September 7ᵗʰ 2018 – My Stay at the Crisis Facility

Today has been an uneasy day. I met with Kim this morning and we talked about discharge plan or what we are doing or where I will go from here.

The building is surrounded. Check the perimeter, my blinds are shut. The doors are locked and are protected by other people. They may infiltrate the building. There is a new client here who must've let in the invisible beings – they possessed them. When will they reveal themselves to me? I am vulnerable – sabotaged.

What and where do I turn to? I will be in charge; I'll take my PRN around 2:00 pm. Everything is OK. I left group due to a client being used as a vessel. How to prove they are real people – time will tell.

Clock is ticking the time passing away. The day is new. The demonic figure made its presence known by showing itself in the bathroom mirror.

September 7th 2018 – Crisis Facility Staff

Savanah slept until about 9am. She attended and actively participated in morning group by completing and then reading aloud what she'd written on the accompanying worksheet. Examples of what she'd written are: This morning I am grateful for: my family, the crisis facility, electronics. Savanah rated her overall mood this morning at a 5/10. Today I will show myself kindness and/or compassion by: Being understanding of myself. Savanah ate lunch with her peers. She attended the 1pm mental health group but left after about five minutes. She later told writer, "I didn't trust the person sitting next to me – she's been taken over by the invisible energy people." Savanah has been visible on the unit watching a movie or socializing with peers during the majority of this shift.

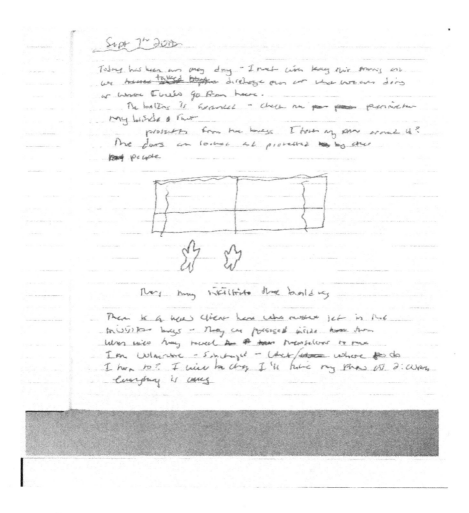

At the crisis facility I found myself feeling uneasy feeling the presence of the invisible people around the building waiting to gain access to the facility to find me.

While at the crisis facility I found myself scared. When one night I went to the bathroom and as I was brushing my teeth, I looked up in the mirror and there he was. A demonic face with teeth bared. I was so scared I had staff check the bathroom for them.

September 7th 2018 – Crisis Facility Staff – 11:40 pm

Savanah was on the unit watching TV at the beginning of the shift. She presented to the nurse reminding her of the "safe word". She received food from her husband at the door for dinner. She ate her dinner at the kitchen table and reported that people eating there "were plotting against" her. Savanah spent most of her time in the living room. She requested the nurse check the bathroom prior to her using it, checking for a "demonic figure". She presented for evening meds and went to bed. Savanah is asleep at this time. Symptoms: **Savanah presented as paranoid and appeared to be experiencing delusions.**

September 8th 2018 – Crisis Facility

I can feel the presence around me in my room. When will he appear today? I am worried about nighttime. It seems he likes to hide in the day but at night he will reveal himself. Its 5:53 pm I took a shower and feel a little better. Mitchel visited me today we talked about workbooks that could help me.

September 8th 2018 – Crisis Facility Staff

Savanah went on a walk with staff and peers. She ate supper and attended evening reflections. Savanah stated she has been working on some CBT (Cognitive Behavioral Therapy) worksheets and learned she likes CBT and thinks it will be helpful to her with symptom management. Savanah took a shower and reported that she found that relaxing and a good distraction. Savanah has needed reassurance throughout the shift that she is safe, and the entities are not entering her peers' bodies with intentions of causing her hurt or pain. Savanah expressed concern that her symptoms have not been getting better with the recent increase her psychiatric provider made to the medication regime. Savanah is currently in bed and appears to be asleep at this time.

I've been working on a symptoms list for my doctor appointment. Staff is helpful, typing up my worksheet, so the doctor can read it better. I'm tired today but it will pass. It's almost 11am and no PRN. Waiting for things to appear. I see them underneath my door. I open the door and they go camouflage. They are teasing me, playing a game, hide and seek. I can see them under through the door. I am listening to praise and worship and it restored my force-field I once had.

GOD IS IN CONTROL. GIVING ME STRENGTH.

I will be in control of the people soon with the force-field. I hear my name being called multiple times. I took my PRN but feel lost. Wandering around. I am unsure of the people the clients/staff. Why are they wanting me to go outside again? Are they waiting for me to confront the beings? Should I tell them to leave me alone again? Maybe they would leave – it's worth a shot.

Early on during my trying times I felt a connection with a higher power. My brain told me that I had a forcefield around me and I could see it, it was purple. I felt like this was given to me by God to show that I am safe with him.

September 9th 2018 – Crisis Facility Staff

Savanah was asleep when this shift began. She woke up shortly after the shift started and attended morning meeting when prompted. She shared that she is grateful for "crisis facility – staff and family" and that today she is going to be patient with herself about "my symptoms if they arise". She shared that an emotion she is experiencing now is "tired/uneasy/unsure of reality" and rated her mood 6/10. Savanah ate lunch with her peers, but again stated that she did not eat much because she did not like the look of the chicken. It should be noted that on the back of Savanah's reflections sheet she made several notes including, "I was able to share because the vessel wasn't here," meaning she felt comfortable sharing her sheet with the group because the peer she believes is the vessel was not in group when she shared. It also said on her sheet "how to tell if they are real? Do I ask questions, or do I leave them alone? Are they real? Yes, they are human, use your skills to understand". Savanah drew an outline of a person similar to a chalk outline and then a more detailed person with arrows going back and forth between them. Savanah met with staff 1:1 today and prepared a list of symptoms for her appointment tomorrow.

September 9th 2018 – Crisis Facility Staff

Savanah ate the evening meal with her peers. She attended group and evening reflections. Savanah shared that she continues to struggle with her symptoms and is concerned that her medications are not working. Following evening reflections, she approached staff to discuss her current symptoms and her concern that the medications are no longer working for her. Savanah was able to list off every medication she has been on and is worried that none of those worked for her either. Savanah discussed her fear that the invisible people are using one of her peers as a vessel to enter the facility. She was able to verbalize an understanding that although she

135

knows her fears are part of her illness, they seem very real to her. She expressed appreciation to staff for being patient and spending the time with her to provide her the reassurance she needs to feel safe. Savanah then decided she would take a shower and retire for the evening. She requested permission to lock her room and requested staff to relock her room when they do hourly checks to help keep the invisible people out of her room.

September 10ᵗʰ 2018 – Crisis Facility Staff

Savanah appeared to be sleeping and breathing during each hourly check of the overnight shift. No concerns are noted at this time; however, it should be stated that Savanah chose to sleep with her door locked due to exacerbated symptoms.

September 10ᵗʰ 2018

Uneasy today because of the staff here and clients. I tell myself do not speak – do not approach – do not provoke. There is a truck outside the building I think they have tracked me through the tracking device in my brain. All I can do is wait for him to leave.

The truck left after a while – not tracking. I am sad because I don't want to be this way. Crying helps, I guess. I don't want to go to a facility again, maybe stay at the crisis facility if I am allowed to. The invisible people are teasing me all day. The voices call my name. I don't want this.

September 10ᵗʰ 2018 – Crisis Facility Staff

Savanah attended morning meeting when her peer that she believes is a vessel for evil/invisible people sat down in group Savanah exclaimed, "Do not speak, do not approach, do not provoke." Savanah spent much of the morning upset and wandering around the building. She felt as though vehicles parked on the road outside had tracked her down and were watching her. Savanah needed a lot of reassurance today. She was also worried that she was going to be hospitalized at her appointment. Savanah was picked up at 12:00 pm by her husband to attend her psychiatrist appointment. She returned from her appointment and reported her medication changes to several staff members and asked if she could/should stay longer. Savanah is currently in her room.

While at the crisis facility I found myself uneasy about one other client. Who I thought was not human and was an imposter trying to get information from the computer man.

September 11th 2018

Today I took my new med, Klonopin. It drugged me up all day, but it happens. Mitchel came to visit today and brought me a movie to watch tomorrow morning. The 5pm Klonopin made me feel tired hopefully I will get used to it. I feel suicidal yesterday/today because of the symptoms once again. I have to sleep it off.

September 11th 2018 – Crisis Facility Staff

Savanah did not attend the morning meeting. She reported feeling too drowsy from the recent addition of clonazepam that was added to her medication regime. She expressed concern about missing programming, but accepted reassurance that staff was understanding of the side effects she was experiencing, and she would not be in trouble. Savanah has spent more time that has been typical in bed this shift. She continues to struggle with thoughts about invisible people or that people are trying to enter her mind when she is on the phone. Savanah is currently taking a shower, something she identified as an effective distraction.

September 12th 2018

Last night I was pukey, so they let me sleep on the couch. I went back to bed around 5am. Today is gone and I'm really tired from the Klonopin. The staff here are really understanding about my symptoms. I felt suicidal because I'm tired of living this way. I have to be unconscious, so I can live. I am listening to music to try and challenge thoughts. I do not want to leave the crisis facility.

What powers do I have? Soon to be revealed. I do not want to die, but it feels like I have already died and am floating in the ocean – next wave coming. I'm paralyzed – sedated but if that what I must do. I will take the sedation over voice/ thoughts/ visions. I am trapped beneath my own life.

September 12th 2018 – Crisis Facility Staff

Savanah seemed quite drowsy after taking her Clonazepam (Klonopin) again this morning. She attended group this afternoon. She continues to ask if staff hear what she hears, "screaming," etc. She has been asking frequently for reassurance and reality checking. Savanah seemed less groggy this afternoon and has received one PRN (as needed) Haldol for reported hallucinations this AM.

September 12th 2018 – Crisis Facility Staff

Savanah was observed watching TV at the start of the shift. She presented to the nursing station several times this evening prior to dinner. She needed continuous reassurance from staff. Savanah appeared "woozy" during the shift and had slurred speech after taking her medications. She did attend group and evening reflections. After group, she went to bed. No concerns noted during this shift.

September 13th 2018

I took my Klonopin I am already so tired, but I force myself to shower, I am unsure about today. They are coming back. I hope Mitchel can pick me up at 2pm. I had therapy and took a cab both ways. We talked about twice a week therapy. Missy was checking to see if I am allowed and Mitchel's mom bought me a cognitive behavioral therapy book. The Klonopin has slowed me down a lot but will get better. I was wetting the bed, drooling, and had slurred speech.

September 13th 2018: Crisis Facility Staff

Savanah was observed on the unit throughout the evening. She ate dinner with peers when prompted. Savanah became extremely paranoid when she observed small children running around outside the building. Staff was able to calm her and redirect her with positive thoughts. Savanah did attend groups, but again had a hard time sharing due to having slurred speech due to her medications. She retreated to bed after group and has been observed sleeping the remainder of the shift.

September 14th 2018 – Crisis Facility

Today has been a good day so far. I'm trying to stay awake for the day. Worried about people's safety.

Positives: made my bed, had breakfast, changed clothes, listened to music.

Negatives: Voices call my name, unsure of reality.

Today someone called me and told me to schedule to see My doctor on Monday the 17th at 12:45pm. I hope it goes well. Mitchel will be there with me. I didn't sleep much as I did before but still drool a bit.

September 14th 2018 – Crisis Facility Staff

Savanah appeared to be sleeping and breathing during each hourly check of overnight shift. Savanah did awake one time around 3:30am to change and launder her clothing due to having an accident in her sleep. Savanah is currently sleeping in her bedroom.

September 14th 2018 – Crisis Facility Staff

Symptoms: **Savanah continued to struggle with hearing voices as Savanah verbalized to writer that "it's pretty much an all-day thing".**

September 15th 2018

We went for a walk today which was nice.

September 15th 2018 – Crisis Facility Staff

Savanah was sleeping in her room throughout the shift. She woke up after wetting the bed but threw her clothes and sheets in the laundry then returned to bed. No complaints or concerns. Breathing and movement was noted.

September 15th 2018 – Crisis Facility Staff

Symptoms: **Savanah continues to share with staff that she is experiencing delusions. Savanah also appears rather fatigued and sluggish as evidenced by her slow speech and verbalization that she feels, "all doped up."**

September 16th 2018

This morning went well, we went for a walk to Walgreen's – the voices are relentless. Telling me not to eat.

September 16th 2018 – Crisis Facility Staff

Savanah was in bed when writer arrived for shift. She did get up and eat breakfast, attended morning group. She is hopeful today to work on her CBT workbook, make a list of things to discuss with her doctor and develop a budget. She stated she was feeling tired, anxious and worried of the future and rated her mood at a 6. Savanah also wrote on the back of her sheet that "today is a good day, command me to do things I don't want to do" and drew pictures. Drew a picture of a tree with a face overhead, the face had a line going top to bottom. On the bottom she wrote, "Everything is Aok cause I'm strong as an Oak." Savanah has also struggled quite a bit today stating she feels "they are out there, and they are coming to get me". She informed writer she has seen them attempting to get through the walls of the courtyard. Savanah has an appointment with her psychiatric practitioner this week and is bringing a list of things to discuss with her psychiatrist. She continued to go between resting in her room with the door locked as she is paranoid someone will get her in her sleep, to following staff around to talk and admitting she feels safe when she's with staff. Savanah understands that her medications can make her

sleepy, she is feeling very drowsy and states it's too much. She is strongly encouraged to share this with her psychiatrist as well.

September 16th 2018 – Crisis Facility Staff

Behavior: **Shortly before the evening group, writer heard Savanah crying in the kitchen. Writer invited Savanah to meet in the conference room and inquired about the reason for her crying. Savanah said she was becoming overwhelmed with the voices because they are mean to her and they don't want her to eat. Savanah said she did not eat lunch today because the voices told her not to eat or she would die. The voices also said that if she ate, other clients would die. Savanah stated the voices call her name, are mean and are very negative. Savanah repeatedly stated I don't want to live like this but also denied wishes to be dead. She added I have a long life ahead of me. Savanah cried for a while longer and shared that she prayed with her brother over the phone. Savanah again said she wanted to eat but the voices are preventing her from eating. Writer offered to sit with her while she eats, and she agreed. She ate a granola bar. She then stated that she wants her psychiatrist to know what is happening to her. She is afraid that tomorrow things will be different, and her psychiatrist will now know that she has been struggling with symptoms. Writer encouraged Savanah to write down what she wants to discuss.**

September 17th 2018

The doctor appointment went well. They discontinued my Haldol and decreased my Klonopin. We will be meeting again on Friday for more med changes possibly.

September 17th 2018 – Crisis Facility Staff

Savanah was awake watching TV with peers at the start of this shift. Savanah met with writer several times throughout the shift. She later ate supper, attended group and shared that this evening she was able to

accomplish what she wanted by preparing for her appointment. Savanah took her meds around 7pm and retired to her room after group. Savanah got up around 11pm to do laundry as she wetted herself in her sleep.

Behavior: **During group Savanah blurted out, "Leave me alone." She was able to remain calm but later asked if she was inappropriate or if she did something bad. Writer assured her she did not.**

September 17th 2018 – Crisis Facility Staff

Savanah presented for morning meds at the beginning of shift. She reported feeling dizzy, so she went back to bed. She awoke at 9 and attended morning group where she reported her intention for the day to be preparing for her doctor appointment. Savanah met one to one with staff. She was transported by her husband to see her psychiatrist at noon. Savanah returned with new medication orders and requested to report these changes to the nurse. Savanah is on the unit watching TV with other clients at this time.

Symptoms: **Savanah reported anxiety over medication changes.**

September 18th 2018

Today I woke up content. Trying to be awake for my meeting with Kim my Case Manager and Rita at 9:15am. I was still a bit sedated/ they are worried about me going home.

We talked about the IRTS but no openings until the end of Oct/early Nov. I don't know if I could make it that long without my meds right. Maybe a home health nurse. I do not want to live in a group home. Feel like my brain is so close to breaking down. I have therapy on Thursday to discuss my suicidal ideation – no PRN yet – no hospital.

September 18th 2018 – Crisis Facility Staff

Savanah has been too ill with her delusional thoughts, speech and reports of visual hallucinations that there are people outside of this facility that are coming to harm her. She needed much reassurance this shift, writer provided time with reality checks with her as well. Although the results are fleeting. She has attempted to sit on the patio with her peers only to encourage them to not have anything to do with her for fear of them being harmed. Savanah is reminded of the time frame she has been here and to consider that nothing has happened, and she is safe here and staff are assuring her safety. She was up about 10:30 pm, she had wet her bed. She was assisted with putting clean sheets on her bed and independently stripped her bed and put the laundry in the wash. She went back to bed.

September 19th 2018

Today I am depressed and thinking about suicide. I don't want to die but if it means they go away then maybe I should do it. The voices/images are showing me dying in so many ways. I am tired of waking up in the night to a wet bed. When will it stop? Too much medication.

September 19th 2018 – Crisis Facility Staff

Savanah approached writer while outside. Savanah reported that she "just wants to die". She stated that the "voices are bad, they are telling me to get the toxins out of my body by cutting my wrist. I just want to die". Savanah reports feeling suicidal and when asked about a plan she stated, "I would cut my wrist." Savanah stated, "I just want everything to stop, the voices and the depression." Writer discussed with Savanah if she could remain safe here. She stated, "I think so." She was able to verbalize that she would seek out staff if her suicidal thoughts increased, or she felt like acting on those thoughts. Savanah discussed the "people that you don't see, they are coming over the walls. They were outside my door last night". She spoke about using distractions to help but feels like the voices are worse than before.

September 20th 2018 – Crisis Facility Staff

Symptoms: Savanah appears to be struggling with symptoms of depression while also experiencing auditory hallucinations as Savanah verbalized that she is feeling like a burden to everyone. Savanah also shared on several occasions what she is seeing regarding her hallucinations and how they are upsetting her.

September 21st 2018

The voices are telling me to kill or harm people – Klonopin saves the day.

September 21st 2018 – Crisis Facility Staff

Savanah took a PRN shortly before supper. She was reporting increased auditory hallucinations. She spent time talking to staff and peers seeking reassurance "until my PRN starts to work". Savanah ate supper with her peers and spent some time on the patio with them. She reported a positive response to her PRN and did appear calmer and more focused. She attended and participated in evening group and evening reflections. Savanah shared that she was grateful for that her PRN had worked and was feeling safe.

September 22nd 2018

This morning has been a good morning. Took my meds, had breakfast and it is getting close to noon and I'm feeling a bit uneasy, but I'm going to wait for my PRN. I am a real person.

September 24th 2018 – Crisis Facility Staff

Savanah was awake at the beginning of shift. She met with staff before dinner to share her poetry. Savanah ate dinner with other clients in the kitchen. Savanah attended evening group where she reported to be grateful for her family, specifically Mitchel. Savanah presented for evening medications and went to bed.

September 25th 2018 – Crisis Facility Staff

Savanah has been up and about during the early part of the evening shift. She attended group and evening reflections. Savanah identified she is working on letting go of worry, stating her life would be good and easy, if she could. She states she didn't show herself any compassion today although she is grateful for her family. She stated she is happy and rated her mood at an 8. Savanah also requested to read some of her poetry to writer, writer has encouraged her to contact places she can submit it for publishing such as mental health newsletters and magazines.

September 25th 2018

This week has been rough with medication changes my doctor added 30mg of Abilify, 50mg Lamictal, 400mg Clozaril, Klonopin. My depression has gotten better with the new medication. I even wrote a new poem about being broken.

Poem:

Schizophrenia isn't a death wish but a life gifted
The voices and visions are not curses but instead an award
Seeing things from all sides
The box remaining unlocked
Slowly releasing toxins into the blood
Darkness infiltrating the mind
The demons take form but soon the light bringers come
And save me from myself
Broken, split, shattered my brain into pieces
Fabric of reality broken
No friction
Nothing to grasp
Slowly slipping
Palms sweaty
Slipping soon

I begin to fall my life flashes in front of me

What a world of make believe I've had

Reality just fiction

Demons, angels, purgatory my life has become a game

I'm slipping under

6 feet

Barely breathing

It has been shown the light

The savior

He will be my protection

Schizophrenia revealed to me what is evil and what is good

I recognize the truth behind the lies

I see what's in store for me

Soon my mind will be empty

Ash from the flame that claims my flesh

One thing stays my thoughts and visions true

Schizophrenia is not a curse if embraced it becomes a way of life

You live with it

Recovery

This poem shows how difficult this illness is because it feels like you're being tormented every day and are waiting for an exit as I was slipping into a deep depression while this was happening. I still have a hard time accepting I have Schizophrenia, so this poem means a lot trying to understand that it isn't all bad.

September 26th 2018

Here I am. My flesh is gone. Burned alive my spirit still breathes. The voices ever present. They yell and command me to stop the burn. Visions of the finished product. Wrists bleeding and body on fire. I get what I deserve is what they say. Soon I will be free. No matter where I go, they follow. They are persistent, but medication helps. It's trial and error-my spirit rebuilding. Powers overtake my flesh and bone are born again. I am strong, it won't be long, I will be gone.

Chapter Nine

Stuck in the Middle

October 12th 2018 – Home

They have taken over my body and my mind. It is not my own. I'm scared when it takes over. Radio says to kill people – visions. I have no free will. I am not alone. Something lives inside I don't recognize. When I look in the mirror. I just see evil. Three people in the yard, I need to run. My free will is slowly draining. I can feel them getting closer to full control. I am not safe from myself; no one is. Where to go? Where to run?

October 26th 2018

They know who I am, but I am in control. No one can stop my powers. I have incredible strength. I can move things with my mind. Last night I was shown a red button and a war. I was told to go there but there are many directions. It could be related. Maybe it will destroy the other people or the computer man. The button must be found at all costs. It holds life and death, depending on who gets to it first.

I can defeat the computer man by finding the button before he flips his switch. He's going to flip it because he wants me to push it and destroy the people. It must be in a warehouse or facility waiting to be found. Who are the followers are they good or evil? Sent from the unknown to aid me in my fight. Maybe this is a war against me. We aren't destroying the computer man we have to destroy myself first.

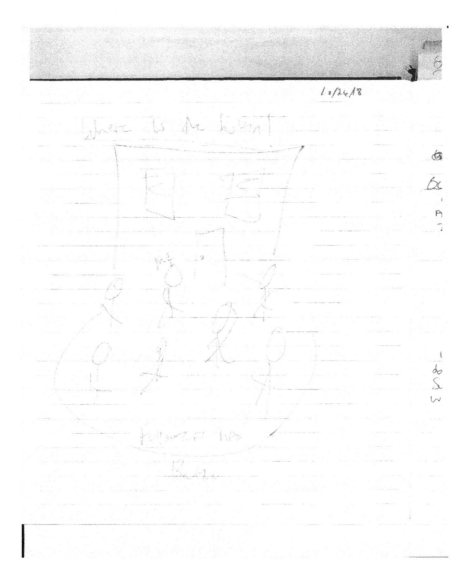

My delusional thinking got the best of me and I was told or shown by my hallucinations that there was an abandoned building waiting to be found. And there was a red button waiting for me to press it and it would bring outsiders in to help in the war, I believed, would come soon.

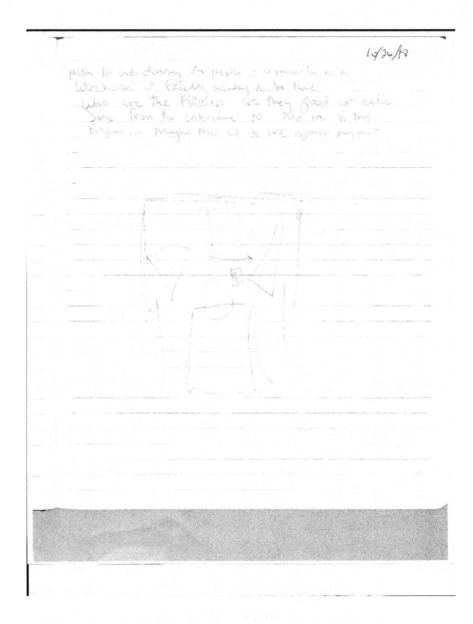

This picture depicts the computer man at his desk showing me on the screens, he was watching me when I was in the hospital, the screens showed the nurses station, my room, and the telephones so he could listen to my conversations.

We are on our way into town and I saw an abandoned building or what looked like an abandoned building. I feel like that is where the button is. Now to find the followers.

How to go about getting to this? To finally be free, nothing hanging over my head. The switch no longer engaged. I feel relief in my head. Something so short, but as night comes so do, they. I have protection over my house. A force-field given to me by God. No demons allowed. Only in the street. I know they wait to watch for me. What if this is what the devil wants? Sending me to a different location to murder me and take my soul?

The demons are trying to lead me, but I stick with the light bringers. I will be safe. I must stay inside. Safe with them.

I AM BLESSED. GOD IS WITH ME.

They are trying to get me on either side. I play a big part in the war about the light bringers and demon/invisible people. The computer man is the devil and the one who put the tracking device in my brain. My faith is what keeps it from being able to be taken over. God will destroy the computer man. I could be the vessel used to kill him and it will end forever.

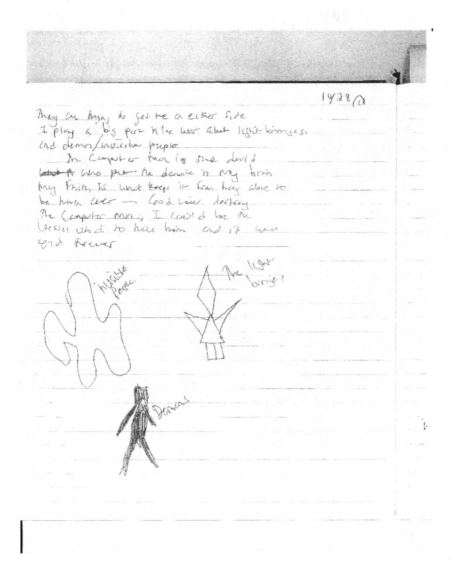

This picture is of the different beings I have seen over the years. They each play a part in the development of my illness. The dark figures are the ones that cause me to be afraid due to how they present themselves. I thought when the "light bringers" came that they would end their reign of terror but instead it was only quiet for a short time. While the invisible people give report and follow me.

October 29ᵗʰ 2018

I feel so toxic my blood feels heavy. I feel weak – I found the possibility that the medication is what's causing it.

You know what schizophrenia causes? It's feeling like a burden when you are sick. Relying on other people to make sure you are safe. It's not wanting to go to a home. It's fear of the unknown. It's recognizing care that support system tries to help. It is having a hard time in the public with something you can't control. Embarrassing. Not deemed safe. That was stripped away. When the illness came it has stripped so much of my life. How to move forward step by step. I'm stripped, I am nothing anymore. What is this life I'm supposed to be?

October 30ᵗʰ 2018

They came through as workers but in reality, it's just vessels from the computer man. While at the IRTS I should have gone to the checkpoint to gather people for the war. The computer man is the one that caused this. I don't have schizophrenia I just need to get to the button to destroy him forever. Defeating him and gaining freedom. I will no longer be a soldier for him. Now to deactivate the tracking device in my brain.

Chapter Ten
Who Will Win?

October 31st 2018

Asking my name? Ha! We'll play a game. Small information given but the spies want more. Who do you work for? The computer man sending messages for me to be sabotaged. They filled my blood with toxins – Lies! Lies! Lies!

All the signs are here for the war. I'm not sure when it will begin but I need to find more people to join my team here. I wonder if I'll be too tired to fight him off that's why I need a strong team. We will be covered in Gods protection. I'm trying to fight me for me. Who is stronger? Trust medication not death!

October 31st 2018

I had contacted the help line to talk because Mitchel was at work. I was consumed with the delusional thoughts of invisible men and people out to get me and soon to track me down.

The help line respondent told me they would call me back with whether I should go to the ER or the crisis facility. They called back and talked to Mitchel about the next step and from the mental health professional they recommended I go to the ER. I went to Madelia Hospital and Clinic to the ER. While at the hospital I was asleep and woken up around 3a.m. to be transferred To a Sioux Falls hospital.

This image is frightening to me still. It shows the blood on the walls at the hospital giving me signs of what was to come. I was convinced that the blood on the walls were what I call the "writing on the walls" which told me that people had died and were giving me information about staff. In the picture I depict the different type of "beings" that I have seen and experienced. The dark figure I refer to them as demonic figures because that is what they look like to me. They are the ones that stand outside my house and watch me. Waiting for commands to attack. The next being is the invisible people. They are ones that watch me wherever I go and appear at times or go camouflage where I can feel their presence but not see them. It's a struggle and confusing but they give the information to the man with no face or the computer man. I found him while I was at the IRTS facility. He was the one that was in charge of the "red switch" which I related to being attached to the tracking device in my brain and if he were to flip it that I would become someone with no free will and do his bidding. They are all terrifying the more I think about them, but it also brings up the question of how complex my brain has become with this illness.

November 1st 2018 – Sioux Falls Hospital

I'm depressed and upset at staff. It is like the crisis facility again. Think positively – you have negative thoughts – why wouldn't I try – I don't think she understands me because she hasn't even talked to me except getting my meds.

Clozaril – 100mg AM 350mg PM

Saphris 10mg AM / PM

Lamictal 150mg

WHAT ARE THESE!??

This image was of the building and helipad at the hospital in Sioux falls. In my mind at the time I believed that this was the abandoned building that was shown in my mind. I thought I had been brought to Sioux Falls to find people who would aid me in a war to come. I was convinced that the red lights were signals for evil.

Signals and sirens. The computer man has come for me, I must warn the others. The signals beeping in my brain. The nurse was very rude and seemed like she didn't care or didn't want me to have the PRN. These nurses are unapproachable and uncaring. They don't talk to you they just sit behind the desk. So far this place sucks and I wish I was at home doing the med change. Maybe I should ask Mitchel to come home.

November 2nd 2018

I heard the beeping noises which put me on alert. I thought they were picking up dead bodies from the night before when we should have evacuated.
    20mg Saphris, 150mg Lamictal, 450 Clozaril

November 3rd 2018

Today has been a good day. Mitchel and his family visited. I miss Mitchel so much, but mom is bringing the boys over tomorrow to come see me. It would be a good thing. Today I experienced extreme diarrhea because I had been so constipated. I was running in and out of group just to go to the bathroom.

I wanted to talk to the doctor about meds, but I had to use the restroom, so I quickly answered questions. Tummy rumbles. I guess there is no doctor on Saturdays, so I'll wait until Monday maybe see about taking them at 8pm now.

November 4th 2018

Today is going OK. I heard the voices telling me not to eat, but I'm going to try and challenge them if they do the same thing at lunch. Mom can't make it, so they'll visit when I get out of the hospital. I miss them a lot and my mom was really sad – I hope the boys don't feel let down.

No voices! No commands! It hasn't been this way for a long time, but I am finally free from the delusional thinking. It isn't real or makes sense.

I get to go tomorrow. Sometime when Mitchel can get off. I'm so happy and excited about going home. I think this medication is good. While there they discontinued my Abilify right away and put me on Saphris 20mg, 10mg in AM and 10mg at bedtime. They also were going to increase me back up to 600mg of Clozapine but with the blood tests it was high, so they decreased the Clozapine to 300mg, 50mg in the AM and 250 at bedtime.

While at Sioux Falls hospital I came to a realization about my illness. I separated the hallucinations and delusions in a chart and wrote down positives of what the cognitive mind would do. It helped for a while until the symptoms came back.

Lamictal was increased to 200 mg in November. At Sioux Falls hospital I was at supper and suddenly, I heard what sounded like sirens. I ran out of the dining room toward to nurses' station exclaiming that there were sirens going off and we needed to evacuate the unit.

The nurses disregarded me and told me to go to my room. I was pacing around the unit and contemplating pulling the fire alarm switch. I then asked the nurse for a PRN Klonopin, but she asked me why I needed it. I was crying and delusional, not making sense. They sent me back to my room after giving me the PRN.

I looked out my room and saw the helipad and the lights were blinking. The next day I was muttering to myself about how the garbage bin outside the windows in the dining room were filled with dead bodies from the night before. One staff member reassured me that there were no dead bodies being taken away. After the episode the next day I was journaling and soon realized that everything I knew for the last three years had been a lie. My brain had tricked me for so long that I wasn't sure what life without symptoms could be like. But now I am free.

At the hospital I met with a psychologist where we talked about the cognitive mind. This was something about getting myself back and living with no symptoms. It was an odd feeling at first living with no voices it was quiet. To help I made a chart regarding the hallucinations and delusions I had and explaining that they can't hurt me and that they are not real.

November 16th 2018

No symptoms and the meds are working. I've been out of the hospital for 10 days.

November 17th 2018

Today is a good day. No PRN'S yet and I'm sitting at Caribou while Mitchel works out. I feel really good on this medicine and I'm more confident in staying home now. I'm not letting my illness take over again. Not like that. I will remain strong.

November 24th 2018

I feel off today. I'm not sure why. Maybe sleeping too late. No voices but delusional thinking. I'm still able to recognize it as that.

November 27th 2018

I feel so off right now – I have to re-live over and over what I'm experiencing. It hurts my brain.

November 30th 2018

Today was a good day. I drove myself to Mankato and went to therapy. I talked about reliving past memories and why they are so intense.

December 1st 2018

We got a lot of snow today – Mitchel and I are just spending the day relaxing. He helped me clean the house by doing dishes. I vacuumed, dusted and did laundry. I want to write a poem, but nothing is coming to my mind. I'm working on staying in control of my mind and so far, it's working. The medication is still working. I feel pretty good.

There is a lot of rage coming back through memories. What is this? What am I feeling? Uncontrollable thoughts. Visions coming in "these decisions are not mine to be made" replaying over and over. They are all coming to get me. I scream for help. Unknown to what I'm feeling. My body taken over, but my mind is not my own. Soon it will be clear again. Medicine helps. The cognitive mind arises. They are just distant memories. Traumatic, but they can't hurt you. You don't have to lose control again.

December 2nd 2018

Today I'm looking back on how ill I was and I'm in awe at what my brain created. For so long I was blinded by psychosis. Years of not knowing who

Savanah was. Now I have had some breakthrough symptoms but nothing unmanageable. My cognitive mind has taken over which is a good thing. I still have trouble with reality, the memories, but they shaped who I am. I need to learn to separate my brain from the hallucinations.

I say they want me to relive this but Missy, my therapist, pointed out that I say "they" in regard to the hallucinations and delusions.

December 5th 2018

I'm uneasy waiting for Tanya at Caribou. There are a lot of people and the noises are difficult to deal with. I am OK. I don't want symptoms to come back. Don't want to take Klonopin but I may have to – not sure. I took a PRN. I'm sleepy, but my brain won't stop. Thoughts infiltrate my mind of an army inside my brain ready to act.

December 7th 2018

Today has been a good day, I drove to St. James to meet with Kim. After that I had to bring Mitchel to Mankato. I went back home and took half a PRN.

December 19th 2018

Tonight, while I was cleaning up my dresser, I found pictures that I drew while at the IRTS. I found them to be a trigger and opened my eyes to the theory of the abandoned building I was inclined to find was actually Sioux Falls hospital where I stayed. The drawings were so similar, so I was stuck in this thinking.

December 26th 2018

Today I met with Tanya and had my blood drawn. I was uneasy right away this morning. I was at the coffee shop for a long time working on my book. I had therapy and saw something 'off' with Missy, but she has been so kind to me. I feel the presence around my house. I am the savior, a beacon of light and hope.

December 27ᵗʰ 2018

Still struggling took a PRN around noon. Unsure of reality. I was OK around 6:00 pm.

December 28ᵗʰ 2018

I'm hearing sirens and the possible presence of beings around here. I must find them.

December 29ᵗʰ 2018

I feel uneasy today – a ball of anxiety but I am listening to music to help. A man is trying to get information through electrical signals on his computer. I have my headphones on to help me protect my brain – how to build a protective wall. No army men since I discredited them. If I don't believe, I have no protection.

I'm waiting at Caribou for Tanya. We need to run and escape the thoughts – leave me alone to the man with the computer. The man with the computer is leaving. He may have breached my wall that was built up. No switch flipped – not real but I feel uneasy like my brain has been infiltrated.

December 30ᵗʰ 2018

PRN 2:47 – ½ tab
I feel off, unsure of what is expected of me whether or not people are waiting for me or if I need to find people.

December 31st 2018

Today was a lazy day but decided to clean up the house to keep me busy – my paranoia is getting the best of me. I took my PRN at 4:00 pm. There were black trucks following me. My mind tells me they are out to get me again. I was able to get my meds but I'm worried. They said it's a different manufacturer. I hope to be able to take them since my brain says it's poison.

January 2nd 2019

My brothers and my mom came to visit yesterday. It went well, and it was nice to see them since they are getting so big. It was a short visit, but better than nothing. Today I met Tanya at Caribou coffee. I was content and calm much less anxious/paranoid than I have been. I didn't need a PRN.

January 4th 2019

I had a couple good days – Today I was uneasy all day. I had therapy, which would have helped but the thoughts are relentless – there will be an ambush at my house. I can't see them anymore, but I feel their presence. what do I do to keep me safe – stay inside? I am unsure of what they want from me. Do I confront them? I know they are in the yard, thousands of them. Do they know I've killed before? I am an evil being more powerful than they know.

January 5th 2019

Today was supposed to be the shopping day for the Boike Christmas, but because of how I've been feeling I stayed home. They wanted to make sure that I was feeling good enough for the actual Christmas on Sunday.

January 8th 2019

Today I met with my doctor and we are keeping the regular medications the same but are adding Propranolol for tremors and anxiety. She also said that if I am really out of it that I could take another Klonopin, but I shouldn't do it every day. She is going to do research about a possible increase for the Saphris since I'm at the max dose right now. 10mg in AM and 10mg PM. I also found out the voice inside my head is a hallucination. I wasn't sure at first, but it is a male voice. She stated a lot of people with schizophrenia have voices in their head. Not my own voice. I guess I have to try and reason with or cut it out. Stop! The thoughts and visions. No one is in my yard and I do not have to listen to the lies.

January 10ᵗʰ 2019

PRN taken at 2:40 pm. The white van tracked my movements and is now parked outside. I'm ready for the attack – my Klonopin is making me tired but I can't let them know or they will infiltrate the building. The beings outside may have been a warning showing me the people where I live and give them access to my home.

January 15ᵗʰ 2019

Had a rough night last night. They were all coming to get me. I told them to stop and to leave me alone. Mitchel was very concerned as I was muttering to myself.

January 18ᵗʰ 2019

PRN taken .5 Klonopin. It's been a rough week. The hallucinations have gotten worse. A male has been telling me to leave my house and find people to help me. I see the wiggly invisible people. There is also a woman whispering to me. I believe these new beings have appeared to frighten me. I can see hundreds of them around my house. I understand that they aren't real, but still tough to differentiate. They are coming back to get – hopefully Mitchel will be OK, and the being will not get him on his way home. I want to make a big sign saying Leave Me Alone! but it might bring attention to me letting people know I am here. 2ⁿᵈ PRN 4:30 pm.

January 22nd 2019

I'm done with my cycle and am feeling better, but I still have to take my PRN propranolol and Klonopin as I get paranoid. The voices have been quiet for a day or so – still confused about going to the old fire station. I still think there is a reason behind this. I was doing OK I took both Klonopin. I was at the store when someone who was behind me became very loud and it made me paranoid and I felt fear that they were tracking me. I ran inside my house hyperventilating and yelling about them coming to get us. Mitchel was really upset and frustrated with me because of my episode.

February 10th 2019

It's been a bit rough lately. My mind has gone on attack mode and has been giving me signals and commands. One of the dark figures that torment me has shown itself and commanded me to go with him. He has electrical powers and a deep voice. I sat in my living room crying telling him to leave me alone. There was no relief. They command me to follow them and go about the town searching for something that isn't there. My brain fighting the best it can against the dark forces. My doctor, doctor B, added a new medication to my regiment. I am now taking Loxapine 5mg in the morning and 5mg at night. The hope is the added medication will help quiet the voices and relieve me of the terrifying visions. Only time will tell if another medication change will help.

February 12th 2019

The medication was not helpful. The hallucinations came back and were more severe. I had to call my doctor about the hallucinations I was having. It began as seeing a dark figure in my living room the being had purple electrical hands. He commanded me to come with him but then showed images of my dad bound in a wooden chair and gagged with a handkerchief. The building where he was being held was someone's house in which I was being told it was abandoned building. When I questioned my husband about the what I thought was an abandoned building, he told me that people lived there, and it was a home. My doctor, Doctor B, recommended that I go to the ER and get placed

165

on an inpatient unit. I went to the ER and got placed at a hospital in Sioux
Falls. I got to their unit by 9:00 pm due to the weather.

February 14ᵗʰ 2019 – Sioux Falls Hospital

This morning it started right away with being paranoid about the nursing staff. I believe the building has been infiltrated with the demons. Soon to take hold of me. Maybe they want to know which is my room unless they use my tracking device in my brain. They can't get through doors. They will play hide and seek. Camouflaging the best, they can hide from me, but only showing the shadows. These men are here to destroy me. A war I thought was won but maybe this is the next step. Soon staff will be taken over. I must fight them off if they turn against me. Only a few to trust. The voices say they want payback for denying their existence and role in my life. How long will I have to suffer until they quiet down. They were provoked and will be sending demons to find me – kill, steal, and destroy. It's what the demons brought them to me. I will have to learn to fight them off. With what powers? There is blood on my hands of the people I've killed. I am evil they say. Good or bad which is true? Will I be forgiven and protected? Ha! No one can protect you! You are ours to play with. My life a game to these beings' control is what they want but the line between reality is blurred. Who to trust only a few will aid in the war? This evening there was a patient who was possessed by a demon. I told the nurses and how security is a big issue for everyone's safety, and we may need to evacuate the unit. They did have the evil one discharged. We are safe for now until they appear again. Cameras can only protect for so long. They will take over. I have no weapons to fight the beings.

February 15ᵗʰ 2019

Increase of Haldol and possible ECT (Electroconvulsive therapy). Today has been OK so far. I'm hoping that I'll figure out what to do about the ECT. The voices came all at one time 2-3 chattering about me. I talked to the nursing students and asked if they were plotting against me. Soon he will take hold. Tick, tick, tick the time will come. Stay inside the house. The voices told me my dad is alive and I need to find him to protect him.

February 16th 2019

The voices are active this morning. They are telling me a war is coming because I provoked them. They will be sending an army to the hospital. We need to group up and train to fight the demons. Chattering 2-3 voices. Is the computer man making his appearance again? maybe he is sending the demons because I deny his existence. Soon to be taken over. The switch will be flipped. If this is truly the work of the computer man, the man with no face. Is he the ruler of the evil one with electrical powers? They are trying to lure me out into the world to finally have hold of me. They say they are coming tonight. I've already been given the premonition of the evil one in my room. I'm not sure what I could do to help protect myself. He is going to try and take me down to hell when I feel like I am in purgatory waiting for judgment. Haldol 20mg.

I am now sure that the computer man has sent the demons. He is the ruler of darkness and I am the ruler of the light. I will soon know how to defeat them using powers given to me. I am unsure of the powers but in time they will be revealed. My brain is not my own telling me there are dead bodies being put into the garbage because they do not have room in the crematorium. I'm not sure who they all have killed. Maybe the dark ones are portraying as vessels. Soon to take over the unit. We will be thrown out like the trash that we are.

February 17th 2019

20mg Haldol. We want to pay a game, hide and seek. We are camouflaged but will reveal ourselves. You must hide so we can find you. When we find you, we will see if he wants us to leave you alone or kill you. It's up to him. Life or death, it's up to him. I'm stuck in the middle of good and evil. A war soon to come we will fight. I don't want to play their game I'm not ready to die. The computer man may be against the evil one and I believe he will soon flip the switch. No free will but ordered to kill. The voices tell me to kill other patients who have the red aura around them. I have blessed my blanket that Mitchel brought me. It will keep as a covering from the demons. It is covered in God's glory.

February 18ᵗʰ 2019

Everything will be OK. Just stay inside the house. I feel uneasy as the demons come closer. They are soon to be on the unit. My blanket will save me but what about the others? How will I save them from the evil one? They are sending in the troops. The unit will soon be overtaken.

February 19ᵗʰ 2019

Today has been OK. I had an uneasy morning and took a shower. I went to music group, but the vessel came in, so I had to leave to be safe in my house. They decreased the Haldol and put me back on Saphris. PRN Klonopin taken.

February 20ᵗʰ 2019

Today I am content. I've been told that my dad is going to come and save me from the evil ones, but he is only given the power through God. He will send them to me. Maybe the light bringers will come back and rescue me from this disease. Haldol decreased and lamotrigine increased. Saphris back at 20mg.

February 22ⁿᵈ 2019

Lamotrigine increased to 250mg. I was discharged and am now taking the same medication I went to the hospital with. This was because the Haldol didn't help even being at a high dose of 20mg. The doctor saw that taking away the Saphris really put me in a decline and so she restarted it and I began to feel better. No hallucinations or delusions today. Before I left the hospital, the doctor had talked about partial hospitalization. The social worker looked around for something close to my home and found P. Care. I contacted them and set up an intake or needs assessment for the 25ᵗʰ of February. They said that they will go over insurance and introduction to their outpatient program. The course of treatment is for three to six weeks depending on how you are doing and its daytime 9-12n so I'm able to live at home.

Chapter Eleven

Closer to Freedom

February 23ʳᵈ 2019 – Home

I'm at home alone today after getting out of the hospital yesterday. It's been a bit difficult trying to start or get back to my routine that I have at home. Being alone is difficult so it's important to keep busy during the day while Mitchel is at work.

February 26ᵗʰ 2019

Yesterday I had an appointment with an outpatient program, and they did an evaluation and I qualified for the program. The problem we had was that they were out of network for my insurance. They couldn't do a prior authorization and I couldn't afford it out of pocket. I contacted my financial worker and she also stated that I can't change my insurance until next year January 2020. I also contacted my case manager, Kim. I am hoping she has other options for me close to home. Today I had my doctor appointment and we discussed the new path we are taking in my treatment. The medications aren't really working for me so they are decreasing and will discontinue the Clozaril. Starting tomorrow I will be decreasing the Clozaril by 50mg each week until I meet with my doctor again on March 19ᵗʰ 2019.

February 27ᵗʰ 2019

I had an episode last night. I lost control and my mind had taken over and I was stuck repeating words. "We are all gonna die!" and, "I have to get out of here!" While I was stuck in this situation I was lying with Mitchel in the recliner. He wrapped his arms around me and was trying to calm me down. He kept repeating my name and when I tried to get up to run, he tightened his arms around me to restrain me. After a while I calmed down and was stuck thinking I couldn't sleep alone because I was worried that they would come after me.

March 3ʳᵈ 2019

Today was rough this morning. I felt off. We are going to Mitchel's parents' house. While there I kept repeating, "I told them to leave me alone." My family had me take my first PRN around 12:30 and another one around 3pm. I was out of it while we were having the family dinner. I was stuck in the repetitive thoughts and continued to ruminate on the sentence. Pacing around, unsure of reality. I couldn't tell what was real or what was fake. I was pretty drugged up but at least I could somewhat function.

March 8ᵗʰ 2019

I've been off this week. Today is the product of days being ill. The demons have told me they are the ones who killed my dad. They wanted blood on their hands and that was my dad. Now the cycle starts again with me. They follow me around making their presence known. It doesn't always have to be seeing them, but I can feel them around my house trying to infiltrate. I was told that I am the queen of the fallen world and this is where the realities blur. Am I good or bad? Light or dark? Am I supposed to go somewhere? Maybe wander around looking for the place to go to meet others like me to figure out the truth behind the demons' desires. Are they here to destroy me and take my life? Maybe that is what needs to happen before the cycle can be cut. It ends with me. The demons will no longer have someone to hold onto or to torture with past memories. I am trying to figure out the purpose of all the beings, who is good and bad. Will the computer man still be sending signals for me and the evil one sending his minions to haunt me? I am not sure what is real and what is not. Am I an actual person or just a robot soon to be told what to do? I'm trapped in my own mind. I feel like I'm being held captive behind my eyes watching someone play me as a game. My actions are not my own. I'm just very confused about what I should do. Do I leave the house or stay inside? I'm not sure where I would end up.

March 12th 2019

Today I met with my therapist and discussed what happened the night before. Monday, I spent the night with voices commanding me to kill my husband or hurt other people. All I could do was sit there and work on coping skills. I tried talking to Mitchel about it, but he was sick and frustrated with me. I am going to be having therapy twice a week this week and will reevaluate on Friday the 15th if I should still have it twice a week. I also contacted my doctor about what happened and my case manager. I wait for their callbacks. My cousin had contacted me after a video I posted about my struggles and suggested I try CBD oil for my hallucinations and delusions. Before I began it, I did research and found that it helps quiet the voices and gives back the feeling of being normal. I bought some at a local store in Mankato.

Chapter Twelve
Finally, Free

March 13ᵗʰ 2019

Today I was waiting for my ARMHS worker at Caribou Coffee. I was feeling uneasy but brought my oil with to try it. I purchased an orange juice since the flavor of the oil is orange. As I sat there waiting, I received a phone call from a nurse from my psychiatrist office telling me to stay on 200mg of Clozaril instead of decreasing to 150mg that night. I believe this was because of the recent hallucinations and thoughts of hurting others. When my ARMHS worker came, I was a little paranoid and having trouble due to the sounds. I decided to try my oil. I put the CBD oil in the OJ and drank it all. It was a bit sour but soon I felt relief and more motivated to get stuff done. The paranoia subsided. It was quiet again.

March 14ᵗʰ 2019

Today was a lazy day. I haven't done much today and haven't stuck to my routine. I decided that I was going to try and go to NAMI support group tonight. While there I met with old friends but soon became paranoid and uneasy about the yelling and banging around from the people playing ping pong at the church where group was at. I sat there ruminating, "We are all going to die. They are tracking us." After a while I became to "out of it" I sat up and told them I must leave because I wasn't doing well. The group facilitator walked me to the door and to let them know when I got home safely. I called Mitchel and he could tell I was not in this world. He had me turn on music and think about the mindfulness exercise I did with my therapist. I got home and Mitchel had my orange juice and oil ready for me. I drank it and took my meds. I was slowly coming back to reality. I asked Mitchel to read the lighted candle exercise and as I breathed in deep and exhaled, I could feel the tension leaving my body and when I opened my eyes, I was back to normal.

March 15th 2019

Since March 13th I have been taking the CBD oil twice a day. I have noticed a difference already and had therapy at 11am. I got to my therapist office and felt content and calm. Missy noticed a big change from how I was on Tuesday to where I am now. She said I wasn't as paranoid, and I was smiling and laughing more. There was just something different. She gave me more homework on CBT and went through the previous homework. I had trouble because I didn't quite understand it but going over it really helped. This now brings me to 12:30 pm when I met with my ARMHS worker. She could also tell I was doing better as she did not have to distract me or used coping skills that session. While together I made a grocery list and meal plan for the week. I was feeling good and went to the grocery store by myself. I haven't been able to do that for a while and while I was shopping, I had no paranoia or uneasiness.

March 19th 2019

Today I am sitting at Caribou waiting for Mitchel to be done working out. My coffee cold as time passes. I have a doctor's appointment today at 2:15pm and will be meeting my case manager there at 2:00 pm. I feel good today! I washed out my hair and put makeup on. I'm trying to do little things to make me feel good like getting my nails done. I think the CBD oil has really helped and my hope is to decrease my Clozaril again. I think my doctor might be apprehensive about it but the last week I have been doing really well. I haven't had to take any Klonopin for over a week. I met with my doctor and she is OK with me taking the CBD oil since it is helpful. I haven't had any voices, visions or delusions for over a week. We are going to decrease my Clozaril by 50mg each month so I should be off of it by July. This makes me happy because I'm tired of taking medication. My doctor also stated that some people have to 'fast' for the CBD oil to still have an effect so if it doesn't work anymore take *a week off and restart it again. I bought some 'gummies' which are like fruit snacks that contain CBD so I can use it as a PRN dose.*

March 20ᵗʰ 2019

This morning I met with my ARMHS worker at Caribou. I'm still doing well we just sat and talked. I also have therapy today at 2:00 pm. I think I'll pass and continue to have therapy once a week since I'm doing well. I'm just so proud and happy to have my life back. I did complete my CBT worksheets for therapy. We are talking about change and that I want to change my thought processes when I have symptoms. I will also ask for more mindfulness and visual imagery worksheets I can have at home to help me ground myself. Therapy went well, I received more CBT homework for next week. I am happy because we are only doing once a week therapy since I am doing well.

March 21ˢᵗ 2019

I had no appointments today, so I felt like being lazy all day. I did have an objective to do though, my ARMHS worker challenged me to go out on my own for a walk. Around 3:30 pm after the cleaning and laundry was done, I went out by myself to the coffee shop and got an iced coffee. I am proud that I did that.

March 24ᵗʰ 2019

Last night was interesting. I haven't felt that way in a long time, but I was in a 'high' or as many know as manic. It started around 6:00 pm and only lasted a few hours thanks to Mitchel. I was so excited and pumped up I straightened my hair and was enjoying music soon feeding into my manic side. I told Mitchel that I needed to clean the house and do laundry. I felt like I was ready to take on the day, but sadly it was nighttime. Mitchel said I could clean until 7:00 pm then I had to take my meds. So, I spent 45 minutes trying to clean and do laundry as fast as possible. After I took my meds I calmed down and fell asleep while watching YouTube on the couch. At that point Mitchel woke me up and went to tuck me into bed.

March 27th 2019

I had therapy today and Missy told me I was a mystery and that I'm just 'Savanah'. The reasoning behind this is because I had a manic day, but no depression. I stated that when it happens, I just get tired the next day and sleep a lot. She said to keep it journaled or monitored to see if there is a pattern. I don't think there is one though. It just happens.

March 29th 2019

Today I met with Tanya and had a good session. We went and got lunch together at Subway. While there I mentioned that I have to figure out if I am a real person. I am just in an unfamiliar situation. Since I started the CBD oil, I haven't had many symptoms so I'm 'normal' or what is normal for me. I am just confused because I don't know how to live a normal life. It has been four years of medication trials, staying at hospitals and crisis facility and a constant battle with psychosis. I am trying to stick to my routine of daily tasks and need to show more attention to my hygiene since it had been a week since I last showered. Since starting the oil, I haven't had a need for naps whereas before when I was taking the Klonopin twice a day, I was sleeping twelve hours at night and then would take a two-hour nap in the morning after being awake for an hour. I have much more energy now and don't feel bogged down by drugs. If I feel uneasy, I eat a CBD gummy and it works to calm me down.

March 31st 2019

Today I took my meds around 8am and went back to sleep with Mitchel until about 10:00am. After I woke up again, I started with cinnamon rolls for breakfast, making coffee, and cleaning up the kitchen. Mitchel got up at 10:30am just in time for fresh cinnamon rolls. After breakfast we went to Mankato and dropped me off at Caribou like usual while he works out. I was feeling a bit off today, but I tried to focus on something other than the feeling. I am still a bit confused on how to live a normal life. Mitchel gets upset with me when I ponder this. He said, "You lived twenty years normally so you should know how to." This is where I get confused because I have been stuck in a rut for years not knowing what is real usually only for a short amount of time then back to symptoms. This new life is one I am happy to discover, but I'm still waiting for the symptoms to berate me again. How do I prepare for relapse? The best thing, I guess, would be to prevent relapse by taking meds and the oil. A part of me wants to stop taking everything to know if I am or that sick part of me is still there. I feel like that is the real me and normal me is just a fantasy I have so longed for. But once again it is unfamiliar. I don't know the social cues of normality.

April 2nd 2019

Today I had a meeting with my case manager at a coffee shop. It went well and we just caught up and talked about how well I'm doing. Later on, in the day I spent most of the day with my father-in-law running errands. We did a surprise stop at a different CBD shop and it was better than the one I went to for my oil. They have their own lab and greenhouse specifically for the extraction of CBD. Mitchel got some gummies that had melatonin in it, and it seemed to help him get better sleep. There isn't much going on lately, but I have therapy and meeting with my ARMHS worker tomorrow.

April 3rd 2019

Therapy went well today. I was a little bit all over the place because I had to do a lot today like cleaning the house. Mitchel left the whole sink filled with dishes for me to wash and put it in the dishwasher. I planned on doing a deep clean of the house and accomplished that task. I felt good after the house and laundry was done. That's where my day went.

April 5th 2019

Today is already a productive day. I had three cups of coffee and started to clean and do laundry. Its 11:30am and am waiting to meet with my ARMHS worker at noon. I've been thinking about the hospital that I used to work at in our hometown. Yesterday I dropped off some scrubs there since I don't need them anymore. I met with my old boss and some of the other nurses. We had a good conversation and I once again thanked them for all their help when I am sick, and I appreciated them. They thanked me because I taught them about my illness and how it can affect someone. Which brings me to think about the past. Last year at this time I was in the hospital in Austin waiting for discharge to go to the IRTS. It is unreal to me about how far I have come within one year. Of course, I started this year off with a hospitalization, but it was for the better and realizing that some medications work better than others. I also have to credit my cousin for giving me information about the CBD. It's been almost a month since I have been taking the CBD oil and have to say it is a life saver. I haven't had symptoms for almost a month and am hopeful about the future. I'm hoping after six months if I'm still doing well, I'm going to see about a job. As of right now my job is still my house.

April 6th 2019

Today was a great day! I started out having my meds and OJ/CBD and planned on going to the new CBD shop called 'The CBD Centers'. When I arrived, I was welcomed by the staff and I was the earliest one to come in. I placed my name in the drawing and won a facial serum and wash. While there I met with a few different employees and told them my story about how I use it for my Schizophrenia and how it helps with symptoms. After sharing my story, I was introduced to Julie, the manager. She loved my story and introduced me to an owner, and they were excited and happy I was benefitting from CBD. After I shared my story to a few people I also told them about my poetry book, and they wrote it down to learn more about me. I listened to the speaker, Josh. He is the grower of the hemp and is from Colorado. He did consults for various places about hemp and the uses for it. He stated that they farm it just like corn and soybeans. It was an educational day as I didn't know much about it but after meeting new people there, I understand more and am going to increase my dose to reach the 40mg dose. Because of the introductions and sharing my story there was a man who wanted to put me in their newsletter. Also, the grower's wife, Nicole, who is in charge of social media would like to do a video interview with me for their Facebook page. I am excited about the possibility of reaching out to other people who have similar issues and introduce them to CBD.

April 10th 2019

It's been a little while since I have written, but I was supposed to meet with Tanya at Caribou but there was a really bad snowstorm. I got to Mankato and it was clear, but I cut the meeting short due to the condition of the roads. I also had to cancel therapy and meeting with Rita on Friday. There wasn't much to do so I stayed home and cleaned the house.

April 11th 2019

Today I have spent a lot of time reflecting on this last year and how far I have come in my mental health. This day last year I had a bad episode in which I began screaming at nothing and filled with uncontrollable symptoms. Now this year, I am productive, keeping my schedule and trying to prepare meals each day. It is a drastic change from being so sick to a functioning human being. I am full of hope and ambition for what my life could be. I have never known so much stability in my life and I'm finally free.

April 13th 2019

Today is an odd day. I get to hang out with my stepmom and sister-in-law, Rachel. We went out to Applebee's for lunch and then went to the mall for shopping. I got a shirt. I felt a bit off but had my gummies with me. I thought it was a fun day we got coffee around 3:00 pm. I took that as a pick me up and began to do spring cleaning at home. Mitchel was playing video games while I went to town on the house. So far, I haven't had many symptoms which is nice. I also showered today which is a big accomplishment for me. I haven't fulfilled my routine lately which brings me into a slump. I feel like nothing is motivating me and I have trouble following through. The shower doesn't have good water pressure, so I find myself washing up at the sink and washing my hair in the tub. I am just apathetic but need to find a way to get out of this hole and begin my life again. Hopefully I could find a reward system for myself for things done.

April 15th 2019

Tonight, it is med time and I find myself taking the Clozaril, and Lamictal fine but when it comes to the Saphris, I find myself unable to take it. It's poisoned is what my mind tells me. Maybe I should take a different one than the one I took out of the package. That one might not be poisoned. Mitchel reminds me that many people with schizophrenia don't want to take their meds but need to do it to function. I'm perplexed. Do I take the advice of my husband who hasn't been wrong yet or do I follow my mind and not take them? I'm not sure why maybe I was overtired and couldn't help the hallucinations of the voices telling me not to take them. Mitchel reminds me that they are not real, but I'm stuck in a loop of telling myself "they need to leave me alone". "I told them to stop." It's something odd that I remember my therapist pointed out to me one time is that I refer to them as 'they'. I have given the hallucinations and delusions person like qualities. I decided to take the Saphris despite my reservations of it.

April 16th 2019

Today was a good day it was beautiful out. The sun was shining so I went for a run to the coffee shop around 2:30 pm. I got home and started the cleaning and laundry before Mitchel got home. He went to work out after work, so I had supper ready for when he got home. I plan on doing a big spring cleaning again tomorrow. I am hopeful for a good day tomorrow when I meet with Tanya.

April 17th 2019

This morning I woke up at 7:30 am getting ready to meet with Tanya at Caribou at 8:30am. It was raining really hard to the point where I could barely see the road, but I made it. We sat down and worked on a meal plan and grocery list. I was uneasy because the CBD oil I have is new to me it isn't water soluble but a tincture that goes under your tongue. I wasn't sure about swallowing it so I've been spitting it out and can tell that it isn't absorbed. I called the shop to see if I could swallow it and they said it was OK. I also realized that I will do what I do with the Saphris and wait ten minutes before I eat or drink anything. We were at Caribou and it was really loud with many people, so I got overstimulated and moved seats. I had to take one gummy to help me out a bit. Tanya and I played rummy to help distract me as a coping skill otherwise I would be stuck in a paranoid state. I am excited for therapy since I didn't have it last week because of the weather. I hope I'll be OK because I still feel a bit off. Maybe another gummy. I also could be off because I'm starting my cycle and I have found that I usually have more trouble during that time. It's time for therapy and I'm out of it. I can feel the paranoia and I am stuck in a thought cycle. So many thoughts to decipher. How to show them what is going on maybe I can transfer information into others. I've tried before but didn't have any luck. I am thinking that there are two people inside me on the left side I have the symptomatic Savanah and the right side is healthy Savanah where they conjoin in my brain. Missy assures me that I am just having more symptoms and has me tell myself that I am having symptoms. After therapy I get more homework and I take another gummy while I'm on my way home. I am home and I am waiting for Mitchel to get off work; I'm stuck trying to figure out my brain. I took a total of three gummies today at different times but by the time bedtime came around I was doing a bit better.

April 19th 2019

I feel better after taking my oil for a few days. I had called to make sure I could swallow it so now I chase it with orange juice. It numbs my mouth after I let it sit under my tongue. I am glad to be getting back to normal after a struggling day. I am clear again and think about how I can help myself out of those episodes. So far, I have no luck except to take the gummies. Today I met with Rita. We talked about how I had a rough day on Wednesday but am back to normal. I did mention that I was questioning whether or not to take the Klonopin now for paranoia if the gummies don't work. She had stated that not to be afraid of it because that is what it is there for. I am skeptical about taking the Klonopin again because I have been off of it for over a month. I am unsure about how it would affect me, if it were to just make me sleep again. Like I said now that I know what a life without sedation feels like. Do I really want to go back? No. I will do my best without it but if it gets serious then I will consider it.

April 21st 2019

Happy Easter! Today we spent the day with my in-laws and went out to eat at Baker's Square. We all got the same food; strawberry crepes and it was great. Jazmin, my dog, is getting a haircut today and Mitchel starts his new shift work tonight. He will be working 11pm-7am this week so he rode home with his parents and went to bed. Jaz looked great but it was kind of expensive. I did well at the restaurant and had a good day. I also decided to take my health into my own hands and am starting carb cycling and doing workouts at home. So far, I created a menu for my week counting the carbs and fats I was taking in. I am hoping this will help me lose weight and get back to a lower weight. I am just happy I am back to normal.

April 23rd 2019

Today Mitchel came home around 7:30am from work and woke me up since he was going to the gas station and to pay a bill. He bought me a Gatorade. I checked my phone and I had a text from my father-in-law and he asked if I wanted to go to Mankato with him to go to Menards. I said yes and took a shower and got my blood drawn and met him at my house. We were gone for a few hours and got coffee together. It was fun and when I got home, I began to clean and do laundry. Mitchel is asleep right now so I can't do some cleaning. At least the dishes and laundry will be done. I am excited for tomorrow for therapy. Last week I gave Missy my book on a USB and am hoping to hear feedback. I am going to contact the crisis facility again about the progress notes.

April 24th 2019

Today I met with Tanya at the mall. We had coffee and walked around the empty mall and Target. It was a good meeting and we talked about my routine and how Mitchel's schedule has affected it. I assured her that things are still going in a good direction and I am completing the tasks of each day. I went home after meeting with her and cleaned up the house while Mitchel played video games. It was 1:00 pm and time to head out to therapy. I am excited today to go through my CBT homework. As Missy and I began talking I'm still struggling with acceptance. I feel when I am doing well, I don't have schizophrenia and that person is no longer with until the symptoms show up. I just am trying to figure out ways to understand it, but once again all I can say is that it is schizophrenia and I have to accept that. I call myself 'weird' a lot because I don't know how to describe myself, but Missy put it in a good way and told me, "You are Savanah, and you are unique." It makes me feel good that I have her to help me through these times but it is also difficult because I feel like I should be able to recognize and rethink during symptomatic times but that proves to be difficult. I tried to explain that I feel like I have two sides of myself and it converges in my brain and they fight for control. Oh well, I guess that is just it, it is schizophrenia.

April 26ᵗʰ 2019

It has been a little while and I received bad news about my new insurance. Because I am no longer on Medical Assistance, I no longer qualify for ARMHS services. Today was my last day with Tanya. We went for a walk down to the coffee shop and had our last drinks and doughnuts together.

May 1ˢᵗ 2019

Today was a big day as I finally met with my doctor since she rescheduled me twice. I was happy and nervous at the same time. I met with my case manager and we gave updates on how things have been going. I filled out my information sheets about depression and other symptoms. The score was the lowest it has ever been. When I walked in to see my doctor, she noticed that I lost weight again and am back down to 145lbs. At the appointment I updated her about how well I have been doing and how much oil I've been taking also asked about the possibility of decreasing the Clozaril. She agreed and I will start decreasing from 200mg to 175mg for two weeks and I have to call the nurse after two weeks and if I'm doing well, they will decrease it to 150mg for two weeks. My doctor said that I will get off the Clozaril but there is no rush to do it. When I met with my doctor, I had Kim and Rita come in with me and they all expressed that they are proud they are of me for how far I have come within the last few months and how much I have changed. My doctor told me

182

that she is happy with the progress and that I chose to run with programs and working hard to control my illness. I told her I have medications, CBD, and working with my therapist on CBT to thank for it. I also gave her the news that I have an appointment for a needs assessment at the Intensive Outpatient Program (IOP) next week on Tuesday. I am sure I will be accepted into the six-week program. Things are finally looking up and are working with me instead of against me. Although there is so much good happening there is still the problem with private insurance so I may not be able to keep my case manager, but I'll know soon. They also said that since I no longer have ARMHS that if I can keep Kim and Rita. That Rita could meet with me each week or every two weeks to make sure I'm still doing well. I am hopeful and excited for the future.

May 6th 2019

It has been rough today. No symptoms but a big wave of depression as I had to put my beloved dog, Jazmin to sleep. She was quite ill and had pneumonia along with heat failure, but she lived a long life of fourteen years. I am sad but know she is in a better place and not in pain. It was hard to say goodbye, but it was best. I do have good news though I get to keep my case manager and Rita. I also meet with Rita this coming Thursday.

May 7th 2019

Today I met with a program coordinator for a need's assessment for the IOP program. I was there for about two hours while waiting to hear back from the doctor. The interview went well, and I received a phone call saying that they accepted me into the program. I am relived and excited but also worried about insurance. I realized how lucky I was to have medical assistance but, this new insurance has some benefits like the covering of the IOP. I have to meet my deductible first. I am sure with my psychiatry, therapy, and blood work it should be easily met. They also have financial assistance where I could get some things covered so I need the forms. Basically, I will only do the program if I can afford it otherwise, I will just stick with CBT at therapy each week. For my therapist if I can't afford it, they do a sliding scale for payments and you pay what you can. Hopefully things will keep going in the right direction and can be afforded. I am happy I can finally say in all truth that I am doing better and functioning. Before there were many times, I thought I was better, but my illness took over but now I am the one in control.

Chapter Thirteen
The End

July 23rd 2019

Today is the day I have been looking forward to for a while. I get to discontinue or get off the Clozaril. I went from 200mg to 0mg in a short time. I am beyond excited to see what will come next. Although I met with the IOP a month ago they never called back to start the program which is OK since my insurance will only cover part of it. They said that most of it will be out of pocket and gave me an estimate on how much the private therapy and psychiatrist would be. I found myself feeling a bit better with my symptoms using CBT.

July 25th 2019

Today was a struggle. I haven't been sleeping well since we stopped the Clozaril. It has become too hard to function on little sleep. My symptoms have come back slowly reaching the breaking point. I stayed up until about 5am. I cancelled my appointment with Missy that was scheduled at 8a.m. today since I was so tired. I never left my house today.

July 31st 2019

I get to meet with Missy today. I am hopeful for a good session. I arrive earlier than usual thinking it would take me longer to get there because I stopped to put gas in my car. I get to therapy and wait in the waiting room until it's my time. As I sit there all I can feel is getting paranoid as the voices start. They want me to leave the building. I struggle as I wait for my time. I talk to myself only fifteen more minutes. Only ten more minutes counting down the time until my appointment. As she comes out to get me for our session, she can see that I am not doing very well. I sit on the couch as my mind goes in all directions. I am speaking rapidly about plans of sabotage by the voices and how they have come for me and have commanded me to follow through with their demands. Then I switch to the topic of what needs to be done today. I am uneasy and not sure of the world right now. While in session Missy calls my doctor and reports that severity of my symptoms as I was actively hallucinating at the session. She only was able to leave a voicemail. While there we made a list together of what to do when I get home. The list consisted of me taking a PRN Klonopin, calling my doctor, doing the dishes and folding the laundry. Usually things that help me cope. I contacted my doctor when I got home and told them of the hallucinations, they told me to wait a few days and call back if the symptoms were still there. They had concluded that it could be caused by the Flexeril I had been taking so I stopped taking it to see if anything were to change.

August 1ˢᵗ 2019

Today I got to see my doctor since the symptoms had increased. I explained the symptoms and the fact that I couldn't sleep. My doctor asked why I didn't call sooner for sleeping medications. I told her it was the weekend and thought I would give it a few more days to see if my body would adjust. It hadn't at all. She prescribed me Trazodone for sleep. I could take up to three tabs which each tab was 50mg. When I got home that evening, I had a hard time after I took my meds. I was so overtired I started to decline as the voices came back. It was all of them at one time again and they began to murmur about me their voices were loud, and I was convinced that they were trying to get into my bedroom through the window. The voices were relentless, and I sat up in bed and began to scream and run out of the room to the front door. Mitchel caught me at the door as I was crying that they were coming to get me. He tried laying with me for me to sleep but I was in episode and couldn't differentiate between realities. He hugged me tight and told me to think about the reasoning behind this. Was it that I was overtired or the fact I went off the Clozaril? It was both. I was finally able to sleep until around midnight where when I awoke, I laid in bed until the morning. The sleeping medications weren't helping very much.

August 9ᵗʰ 2019

I shouldn't be driving is what Mitchel says. I am a danger to people on the road because of how ill I am. I tell him I have appointments to fulfill as I have waited for my yearly physical for almost two months. I drove to a clinic to have my physical and check up with a female doctor. While there I began to feel uneasy as I changed into a hospital gown waiting for the doctor to come in. I told myself to be good and remain calm. As the doctor entered for my exam, I began talking about things that needed to be done around the house and what I was going to do later. As the symptoms began to increase, I started to say my normal lines. "Everything will be OK just stay inside the house." The doctor became concerned as I kept repeating this phrase. When the exam was over, I got dressed and ready to leave. I was paranoid and was unsure of what to do. As I left the room the doctor asked if I was OK. I replied, "I'm ok, I'm always ok." I walked out to my car and talked to my mother-in-law about how I was feeling off. I just have to make it home I thought to myself. I drove home in a daze and when I was home, I took a PRN Klonopin. As I sat in the living room chair with nothing on my mind was going wild. Then I received a text from my mother-in-law saying, "It's such a nice day out!" After receiving this text, I decided to sit outside on my front doorsteps. While sitting there I began to have command voices telling me to walk but giving me no destination. I had no shoes on, but I began to walk doing what they said like a robot. As I approached a corner of the block there were some teenagers getting ready in a car when one approached me. She asked if I was OK. I told her I was unsure of where to go and that I was lost. Also, that "they" were telling me to walk. The girl told me where the police station was, and I said I would walk there. I got about another block away and then remembered that I had a cell phone. I then called my mother-in-law stating I was lost and had left the house with no idea how to get home. She pulled up google maps trying to find out which street I was on and how to help me get home. While on the phone she told me, she would hang up and call the police to come and get me. I stood at a street sign waiting for the police when she called back. I told her that I should keep walking and that I saw a red truck like Mitchel's on main street. I thought I should meet him there, but he was still at work. About a block away I see the girl who talked to me they were waiting and watching me as they had also called the police. At that time, I was still on the phone and the policeman came to my location. I gave him the phone and my mother-in-law told him my address and he then took me home. The sad thing is I was only a block away from my home, but I was so disorientated that I didn't realize it. The policeman stayed with me until Mitchel got home and he asked me if I was taking my medication and at that time, I explained about stopping the Clozaril and that I had a doctor's appointment on Monday. He suggested the crisis facility, but I told him I should be Ok at home with Mitchel.

August 12th 2019

Today is my doctor appointment. Kim or Rita couldn't be with me, so Mitchel took the day off to go to the appointment with me. At the appointment I told my doctor of the symptoms I had been having and she decided that we should restart the Clozaril. She also had me stop taking the CBD oil and gummies. After my appointment Kim and Rita called me to where I explained everything that has happened lately, and they suggested to call the crisis facility. I agreed but Mitchel was skeptical because I was having such a good day. I did what I was supposed to do and called the help line they came to my house for an evaluation. When they arrived, I was honest, and they decided that they were going to admit me that night. I packed a bag and got ready to leave.

August 13th 2019 – Crisis Facility Staff

Savanah was awake and in the dining area when writer arrived at 8:00 am. Savanah willingly participated in the morning program. She shared that her challenges/symptoms she was experiencing were "confusion". She rated the symptoms as a "6" out of 10. Signs of Symptoms: Savanah approached writer several times throughout this shift and appeared to be confused and scared. She shared that her auditory hallucinations are leaving her confused "and they won't tell me what to do". On one occasion Savanah was reduced to tears due to the intensity of the symptoms she was experiencing.

August 13th 2019 – Crisis Facility Staff

Savanah agreed to meet with writer 1:1 to discuss auditory hallucinations and paranoia, and coping skills for managing these mental health symptoms. Savanah rated the intensity of her auditory hallucinations, paranoia and delusional thinking to be a "7–8" on a scale of one being the lowest and ten being the highest. Savanah was responding to internal stimuli throughout the 1:1 meeting. Savanah reported her "voices start talking, inserting thoughts and images to my brain". Savanah reported worrying about "my brain isn't right and I'm scared I'm going to lose control again". Savanah did the reality checks. These are important to her because the voices tell her to do the opposite. During the meeting Savanah's mood appeared to be fatigued and her affect was flat, and congruent with her mood as demonstrated by limited facial expressions during meeting, not talking due to distractions from internal stimuli. Savanah would also become tearful when discussing her concerns about not getting better. After the meeting Savanah took a PRN, took a shower, and had a cup of tea. After engaging in these self-care activities Savanah's mood appeared to be euthymic and her affect was congruent with her mood demonstrated by herself report, being more talkative, and exhibiting normal range of facial expressions and engaging with staff at group.

August 14th 2019 – Crisis Facility Staff

Savanah was awake and in the dining area when writer arrived at 8:00 am. Savanah participated in the program including morning meeting. During the meeting Savanah agreed to fill out the form but declined to share. However, her morning meeting handout stated that some of the challenges/symptoms she was experiencing were, "I am very tired and uneasy." When asked to rate her symptoms on a scale of 1-10, she rated it a 6. She is going to cope by "sticking to my list and talking to staff". Her goal for the day was to "manage symptoms as they rise". Signs of Symptoms: Savanah appears to be struggling with a multitude of mental health symptoms including auditory and visual hallucinations along with paranoia and anxiety. Savanah approached writer several times during this shift requiring reality checks as she is wanting staff to be posted around the perimeter of the facility to ensure her safety.

August 15th 2019 – Crisis Facility Staff

Savanah was awake and in the common area of the facility when this shift began. She is attending morning meeting and shared that she is feeling very uneasy and "a little off". She requested a PRN this morning in what she stated was an attempt to hold off the voices. Savanah has interacted with staff throughout the day to engage in reality checks, gain assurance for her safety and to request assistance with distractions from her hallucinations. She reported some paranoia following lunch that she was not sure if the staff were real or not. Savanah was reassured when she learned that she could ask to see staffs' name badge if she had any questions. Savanah reports she is looking forward to receiving a visit from her husband this evening.

Writer encouraged Savanah to engage in reality checks when her auditory hallucinations and paranoia begin to increase, and remind her of the three things she identifies as helping with these checks:
-It was my plan to come here
-It is a safe place
-I am a good person
Writer encouraged Savanah to seek out staff if she needs anything throughout the evening.

August 15th 2019 – Crisis Facility Staff

Writer has interacted with Savanah multiple times this shift to discuss her hallucinations and paranoia. Writer has provided reassurance, encouraged the use of distractions, engage her in reality checking and assist her with her laundry. Savanah reported that the voices were telling her to walk but would not give her a destination which was causing her to become anxious and scared. She identified coloring as something she could do to distract herself from the voices but indicated that she is waiting for a text message from her husband who usually texts on his work breaks and she planned to focus on that. Savanah again approached staff reporting that she was tired but afraid to go to sleep in case something bad happened and she might not hear it. She accepted staff's reassurance that the alarm system here was very loud and that staff would also seek her out to assist her. Savanah again approached staff to report that she was feeling like someone was coming after her and she did not feel safe. She agreed to work on completing her laundry then to just spend time sitting with staff so she would feel safe. She also reported some paranoia about staff and her ability to determine if they are real or not. Savanah shared that she understands the voices she is experiencing them and has difficulty reality checking without staff assistance, reassurance and encouragement.

August 15ᵗʰ 2019 – Crisis Facility Staff

Savanah agreed to meet 1:1 To discuss her experience of auditory hallucinations, paranoia, and coping skills to effectively manage her symptoms. Savanah reported, "I've had a hard day today." Savanah explained she has been struggling with her auditory hallucinations and paranoia, and that her symptoms had been so intense that she had already taken her two PRNs for the day. Savanah's symptoms of auditory hallucinations and paranoia were not present during the 1:1 meeting, and there was no evidence of her responding to internal stimuli. Savanah was engaged and talkative during the meeting and shared a lot about stories about how her mental health symptoms affect her daily life. Savanah reported worrying her symptoms will become too overwhelming in the future and that she might lose control of her brain. However, Savanah also reported she is going to keep trying to work through them and expressed being hopeful that her medication regimen will get "figured out" so her symptoms become stabilized. Shortly after the 1:1 meeting had ended Savanah approached writer appearing to be responding to internal stimuli. Savanah reported being worried that one of her peers "was not a human" and that he "was an imposter". Writer collaborated with Savanah to do a reality check, and this appeared to help decrease her symptoms. During the 1:1 meeting Savanah's mood appeared to be euthymic and her affect was congruent with her mood as demonstrated by her self-report and being positively engaged during the discussion. However, after the initial meeting, Savanah's mood appeared to be anxious and paranoid and her affect was congruent with her mood as demonstrated by her responses to internal stimuli and being worried that one of her peers was not human.

August 16th 2019 – Crisis Facility Staff

Writer met with Savanah. Savanah was tearful and began a tangential thought process regarding her hallucinations. After Savanah calmed down some, she agreed to walk back to the office with this writer since the office does not have windows. Once in the office, Savanah became very upset and backed herself into the corner. She cried very hard, was hyperventilating, and was yelling at the things she was seeing and hearing. At first, Savanah was unable to utilize reality checks to reduce these symptoms. Savanah would not look at staff directly and kept repeating, "I am a good person. Why do they keep telling me I am a bad person? They are telling me I deserve to die. I know something bad is going to happen tonight. They are going to break into the building to get me. If I try today, they are not real, they will retaliate against me, so I have to believe they are real." After some time, she agreed to walk to her room and use her weighted blanket. She then suggested that she take a shower to "pull her back to reality". While this episode was occurring, Savanah rated her symptoms at a 10. After using reality checks, she rated her symptoms at a 6. Savanah was responding to internal stimuli, including voices and seeing the "invisible people" for approximately half of this meeting.

August 16th 2019 – Crisis Facility Staff

This writer interacted with Savanah throughout the day, including sitting by her as she colored to reduce delusions and help her distract. Savanah shared that distractions work best for her like talking to people, coloring, taking a hot shower, and playing on her phone. She also reported sensory things help her too like her weighted blanket, a hot cup of tea or even holding a cup of hot water. Savanah was having a hard time staying in the now and thought there were "the invisible people out to get me". She stated they were outside and trying to get in and she could hear them talking to her. Savanah also stated that there was a peer here that she did not trust that was infiltrated and trying to get her information. Savanah agreed to color next to writer to distract her from her own thoughts. Savanah rated her symptoms a 7-8 out of 10. Savanah appeared anxious as she rocked at times and looked down and her eyes paced back and forth. Savanah spoke in a quiet voice and made occasional eye contact. Savanah appeared to struggle today with delusions as she would back up talking to herself, "they are going to get me," "I can hear them talking," "they are going to get inside." When she colored, it helped her for a short time not talk about her delusions as long as she was redirected frequently.

August 17th 2019 – Crisis Facility Staff

Savanah approached writer to talk several times during this shift. Savanah had endorsed that at times she doesn't feel safe because there was only 1 staff near the front entryway as she was concerned that "they are going to come in and get us. All of us. Are we going to be OK here?". This happened 3–4 times throughout the duration of the shift. However, at other times Savanah would sit and speak with writer and seem to be experiencing minimal symptoms. When discussing coping skills, Savanah shared and did the coping strategies she said she would try with writer such as playing a game on her phone, sitting in the common areas of the facility and talk with peers, drink tea, and call friends and family. After utilizing her strategies, it appeared to alleviate symptoms, but for not a long period of time. Savanah appears to be struggling with a multitude of mental health symptoms, including increase in paranoia, hallucinations, and delusions.

August 17th 2019 – Crisis Facility Staff

Writer began the evening shift at 4:00 pm and was asked by another staff member during shift change to intervene with Savanah because her mental health symptoms of auditory and visual hallucinations, paranoia and delusional thinking were significantly increasing. Writer intervened, and conducted reality checks based on the previously documented points of:

- It was her plan to come here
- The facility is safe
- She is a good person

These points are emphasized during reality checks because Savanah reported her auditory and visual hallucinations attempt to convince her of the contrary. From approximately 4:00-5:00 pm Savanah would not leave the great room meeting table, reporting, "They won't let me leave," and, "if I leave from this area, they will retaliate against me." Savanah also reported, "They want me to leave the building and I don't know what to do." Writer continually reminded her of the reasons for coming here and that she was safe. At one point, Savanah began to crawl into the chair she was sitting in and appeared to be trying to get away from something she was seeing. When this occurred, she began to cry, take short breaths, and was responding to internal stimuli saying "what did I do to deserve this" and "they are here". Savanah also began to cry, saying, "They aren't going to let me eat. I am so hungry, but they aren't going to let me eat." Savanah took her PRN at 5:00 pm, which was her third for the day. She attended supper with her peers but sat alone and was responding to internal stimuli. Writer attempted to conduct reality checks with Savanah while she was eating her meal and she continued to state, "They are telling me I can't eat, and I just want to eat." Savanah was crying and repeating this statement while taking bites of her food. After dinner Savanah reported to take a shower, which has helped her with symptoms in the past. After taking a shower Savanah took her evening medications at 7:00 pm, sat in the Great Room commons area, and eventually became symptomatic. Savanah stood up and appeared to be responding to internal stimuli. Her affect appeared to be horrified by what she was experiencing and began to say, "They are in the building, they are here. I need to get out of here." While Savanah was responding to internal stimuli, she was slowly walking backwards into the corner area of the Great Room as if something were approaching her. Staff attempted to approach Savanah to conduct reality check and try to calm her down. Savanah responded by running away to the East Wing of the facility. Three staff, including the nurse, followed her to the East Wing to try and calm her down. While these three staff were with Savanah, writer called the Mental Health

Practitioner on call to discuss potential options for higher level of care if Savanah did not respond to interventions. MHP stated to continue on working to calm Savanah down but if she was unresponsive that staff should call the police escort to take Savanah to a higher level of care at the hospital. The three staff were able to intervene successfully, and Savanah eventually calmed down. Although calm, Savanah was still symptomatic as indicated by her need to have staff check her room to ensure it was safe from the "intruders" she is experiencing due to internal stimuli. Savanah went to bed around 7:37pm.

August 18ᵗʰ 2019 – Crisis Facility Staff

Savanah approached writer and addressed her concern with "how I was last night". She stated she missed group because she feels too "paranoid to sit at the table with everyone even though I trust them". She shared with writer that she tried a hot shower as a distraction and "it helped a little". When trying to brainstorm other coping strategies, she replied, "I don't know anymore. I've been trying to figure out something that will work for four years." However, Savanah did acknowledge that if she is able to recognize warning signs sooner, maybe the intensity of her "break downs" will decrease. Savanah's symptoms at this time appear to have decreased. However, Savanah's symptoms have seemed to fluctuate throughout the course of the day, for the last several days.

August 18ᵗʰ 2019 – Crisis Facility Staff

Savanah was in her room sleeping when writer arrived at 8:00 am. Savanah completed a morning meeting handout but elected to not share with the group. Later in the shift, Savanah's symptoms appeared to be increasing. Therefore, writer and Savanah met and discussed her symptoms and her safety here. Savanah explained that she feels like "I'm getting worse and there's not much anyone can do here. I'm scared because these voices are getting scary and meaner". When asked to elaborate on her voices, she stated that her voices are telling her to hurt herself and/or someone else and that she doesn't want to do anything to anyone but is worried that "the voices might win". She also explained that she has been trying to utilize her PRN's, "but they're not doing anything at all. Last night was terrible and I'm so scared it's going to happen tonight because I'm not getting any better." Throughout the time she was speaking with writer she appeared to be responding to internal stimuli while also crying to the point where she was unable to speak. Savanah eventually agreed that she may need higher level of care and thought it was a good idea for her to go to the ER. Savanah's husband will be taking her.

August 18ᵗʰ 2019

Today at the Crisis facility, I reached out to staff because I haven't been doing well. Last night I had an episode where I was seeing the invisible people and that staff didn't look like real people. They were approaching me, and I was backed into a corner. I then began to tell them to get away from me as I ran through the building to the other lounge. I was shaking in fear and I had taken all my PRN's for that day. The Klonopin was no longer helpful. We had called earlier on Friday for an increase in the Klonopin or a different PRN but, my doctor said she wouldn't do anything until she saw me. I was stuck on the back burner with her. When I talked to staff today, I told them that the voices and beings were implanting thoughts in my brain to kill the other people in the building. At that point they had talked about me going to the hospital. This staff member allowed me to take a shower and do laundry before leaving for the Emergency Room in Mankato. I called Mitchel and asked if he would come pick me up and take me there. He agreed.

As I entered the hospital's ER, I was having trouble concentrating and going through the motions. I have been here before. They took my vitals and then escorted me to my room where I met my nurse and doctor. The social worker had received paperwork from the Crisis facility, so it was nice not having to explain things. Mitchel was there with me. I told the staff the voices were telling me to leave the building. At that point the doctor stated that if I tried to leave, they would put me on a 72-hour hold. Six o' clock came around and I had eaten my supper and convinced Mitchel to leave to go back home since he had to be up the next day for work. As he left, I was there alone with voices and intrusive thoughts. I began to be consumed with delusional thinking and thinking that the invisible people were in the ER with me and that I needed to protect staff. I began to do as the voices said. I walked out of my room to talk to staff who told me I needed to go back to my room. I did. Back in my room I began pacing around and talking about the invisible people and how we needed more security. I wasn't making much sense and that is when "it" happened. The Social Worker, doctor, nursing staff and security were all in my room. They told me to sit down in a chair that was there. I sat down and saw that the nursing staff had two needles. At this point I was confused and was yelling telling them I did nothing wrong and that I was scared that they were trying to drug me and put me in a facility. When the nurses with the needles came in, security held my right arm down and another nurse held the left arm. I was stuck and that's when the two nurses stuck one needle in my left thigh and the other in my right thigh. The medication hurt and this was my first Intramuscular injection. The medications they used were Haldol and Versed. They told me I would sleep soon and helped me to bed. At around 11:30 pm shift change came, and I was as awake as I could be and took my nighttime medications. I heard part of the shift report talking about me and the had stated that I was just worried about people's safety. At 9:30 pm, I was put on a 72-hour hold. It wasn't until midnight that they found placement and I was going to be sent to Albert Lea.

August 19ᵗʰ 2019

It's two o' clock in the morning when I arrive and fill out the necessary paperwork for the unit admission. I am then taken to my room where I try to get some sleep. It is 7:15am and breakfast is here. I got little sleep except when they gave me the shots in the ER. My thighs still hurt from them. I was confused and consumed with the delusional thoughts and hallucinations of the invisible people. I go over to the other side of the unit where they eat. I was nervous and talking to myself about possibilities of the invisible people using other patients as vessels to soon kill me. I felt the need to arm myself and soon found that the command voices were back. The thoughts that came along with them were disturbing. I felt like there was a microchip implanted in my brain and that is how they were controlling me. After breakfast I met with Dr. R who was my doctor. They had just moved facilities. As I sat in his office, I remember him asking various questions about me but, all I could do was speak rapidly about the invisible people and that we needed security up here. And that I was told to kill either other people or myself. I asked for the blueprints to the building so I knew which exits needed to be covered by staff that would allow us to be safe. The doctor said, "You have a lot on your mind." As he kept typing and soon, we were finished, and I was sent back to my room where they then closed the door leading to the other side of the unit. I spent most of the day not in reality and the nursing staff had to help ground me and told me I was OK and in a safe place. I was in fear of what I was seeing but I was then put in my room for quiet time which helped. At this time, I am on 50mg of Clozaril since the last time I saw my doctor and we were going to increase it every four days but now it's different in the hospital.

One thing that surprised me the most is when the social worker came in and handed me papers about a Civil Commitment. The doctor had filled out a Petition for Commitment on me due to my mental illness. The reasoning behind the commitment were as follows: Behavioral evidence to support commitment were – Auditory Hallucinations, Command hallucinations to kill others, suicidality, fear of space vessels. Patient is a risk to self or others due to: Suicidality. When served these papers, I became very angry cause I felt like I did nothing wrong and that it was a punishment for me being ill again. It wasn't until later that I realized the staff were just looking for my best interest. While I was still processing this, I called Kim, my case manager and explained that they wanted to commit me. She said that two of her coworkers who do the pre-screening had left and were going to meet me that day. Two ladies from my county came to interview me. I was glad they caught me at the good time of day for me. When they arrived, we met in my room where I had to explain what lead up to the hospitalization as I was telling them one of the ladies stopped me and told me whatever I say can be used in court if they pursue commitment. I understood but, I was trying to be as honest as possible but without going into too many details. As I was talking one of them was writing down what I said as they asked questions. They were very nice people and told me that I would be hearing from them in a day or two regarding their decision. I signed a release of information so they could speak to my family, case manager, CSP, and contact the hospital records department. I was nervous for the decision.

August 20th 2019

Today I woke up anxious as the day went by waiting for the dreaded phone call. Early morning, I received the call from the county, and they had told me that they were not in support of the commitment. I was ecstatic and full of relief I didn't want to spend a part of my year being in a facility again since I had been doing so well before. Later in the day the county sent over paperwork explaining their decision and had stated that I had a good support system and insight into my illness. Although that was the good news, they also stated that if symptoms were to increase or become more severe, they have the right to pursue commitment.

August 20th 2019

I talked with the doctor today and we are going to increase my Clozaril to 100mg instead of moving up to 75mg. I asked if we would increase it anymore during my stay here to which he replied that we would revisit on Friday. So, I waited and found out that I would be discharging Sunday the 25th of August at 11:00a.m. I was excited but worried at the same time. The paranoia kicks in as I wait for the meds to work. I'm still consumed with the fact that the invisible people may have been let on the unit using other patients' as vessels to come and kill me. I express my concerns with the nurses, and they assure me that I will be safe and that they have a direct line to the police and security.

August 22nd 2019

Here it is again the voices are back. I need to arm myself at supper time for the war to come. All I have are plastic utensils and Styrofoam plates due to the severity of the hallucinations. I tell the nursing staff of the microchip that has been implanted in my brain and that is how they are commanding me to do things. I am a robot I say. I have no free will. I have begun to talk back to the voices and asking them questions. Like when I was at the Crisis facility, I asked them if I was allowed to get a drink of water or to eat my meal. They are relentless and soon I am overcome with the inability to make my own decisions. I tell the staff we need to call the police because the invisible people are on the unit and we must evacuate the building for our safety. I once again ask for the blueprints to the building to find a way out. The one nurse who told me they have a direct line to the police was in the right mind. I told staff to call the police to come and monitor the situation with the invisible people and vessels. They said no but they would keep an eye out.

August 23rd 2019

Today we have a fill in doctor since Dr. R is on vacation. Him and I had a plan to revisit increasing my Clozaril today, but the new doctor has no idea what is going on. She came to visit me in my room for less than five minutes. I began to tell her about the symptoms I was experiencing, and she stated, "You know they're not real, right?" After that she got up and left as I asked about increasing the Clozaril. She found me later in the day and told me we would not be increasing it since there is little time and that I could probably get off the Clozaril. I was astonished that she had said that to me because that was the whole reason I was in the hospital. Everyone on the unit came to a consensus about the doctor saying that she had no idea what was going on and was rude. I was worried about what she would write about me due to the lack of conversation with her. I didn't want her to write a large summary on the five minutes she was with me. After the meetings I was really frustrated and angry because Dr. R and I had a plan about my medication and now I have to wait for the weekend doctor. I wanted an increase today because that would give me two nights and three days to see how well it works and that they could monitor me before I go home.

August 24th 2019

It is one day before my discharge. I am sitting in the community lounge on the larger side of the unit with new friends I have made. They invited me to play UNO a couple days ago and now I spend most of my time with them. I begin to have trouble around 6:00 pm. The thoughts are coming back and so are the voices. "No Savanah!" I say. "You don't have to tell them anything, I told them to leave me alone." "They know I am here." I am stuck in the rabbit hole. Going downhill as I speak to the voices. As 7:00 pm. comes I go to my room to take my medicine as Dr. S (the weekend doctor) had increased my

Clozaril to 200mg at bedtime. I told the nurse about the microchip in my brain and how it has affected the tracking device that they are both trying to control me. She asks if I think I should go home tomorrow to which I reply, "Yes."

August 25th 2019

Today is discharge day and I am ready to get home. Mitchel will be here around 11:00a.m. to pick me up.

August 26th 2019

Today is my first day home from the hospital. My family has been checking up on me to make sure I am ok. So far it has been a good day I was able to sleep in until 8:30a.m. It was nice not being woken up at 6:30a.m. for vitals or at 7:15a.m. for breakfast. It is kind of nice to begin again back on a higher dose of Clozaril. I'm hoping that my outpatient doctor will keep me at 200mg or higher from now on. Now that we know that the medication was doing its job, I don't plan on making any changes to my medication ever again. When I am doing really well, I'll need to remind myself of this past month and how severe my illness can get when I take away even one medication. I believe I will probably be on this combination for a while and will become stable again. I am still glad about the trial and error we did with the Clozaril because if I didn't try, I would have never known that the medication was working. I am just thankful for the staff at the Crisis facility and the hospital which helped me get better. I am hopeful for the future.

August 30th 2019

I was doing well but the symptoms came back again. I decided to call the help line to see if I could stay there again while my medications are getting figured out. The Crisis facility suggested I go to the ER and to seek inpatient treatment. They told me not to go alone and so I called Clare and she was able to leave work on her lunch break. When she arrived, we then went to the ER. I knew I would be treated good there because they wouldn't give me any IM injections. While there I spoke with a doctor and he said they would be looking for placement for me. I was hoping to get back to where I was there a week earlier. I regret leaving but here I am again in the ER. Mitchel came to sit with me until about 7:30-8:00 pm. Clare left, and I took my medications and Mitchel tucked me in the hospital bed and left. I was woken up around 10:00 pm for transfer. My brain wasn't working correctly but I had a good EMS team. It was about a two-hour drive to Owatonna where I was placed.

September 3ʳᵈ 2019

Today was a difficult day. It started with voices calling my name which lead into paranoia and stronger hallucinations. I was repeating, "They are coming for me tonight. They're going to kill me!" while I was in episode no PRN's were given and I sat down with the doctor where he asked me questions about my life which helped distract me. Distraction is key when dealing with me. Although I calmed down, he stated that he had "some thoughts" about my MMPI-2 which is a psychological exam. It came back invalid, but he still interpreted it anyway. While in this meeting I didn't like how he wanted to paint myself victim by saying, "Poor Savanah." I told him I don't take pity or like it when people just see me as "sick Savanah".

September 4ᵗʰ 2019

Although I left the Albert Lea hospital angry with my mom, she really stepped in wanting to be a part of my support system. She made sure I had a visitor each day and even brought my brothers. I was worried before, but I feel like this conversation may continue outside of the hospital. I saw my uncle Jay, mom, Gunnar, and Liam. They have gotten so big now almost teenagers. I did enjoy having visitors and being with my family again. I am glad to be going home soon this stay hasn't been the greatest. I didn't really like the doctor or things he had said to me but on the bright side I am up to 300mg of Clozaril. I should be feeling much better soon.

October 5ᵗʰ 2019

I am back to being a normal functioning adult! Since I left the hospital, I have been stable and am even going back to the gym every day. I am working toward my goal of losing weight and so far, I went from a large size pants to a medium. I have a doctor's appointment on Oct. 15ᵗʰ which I'm worried about because I still have a head bob and she wants to take me off of the Saphris to see if it will help. I will have to think about it because is it worth ruining a couple months to see? I will wait until I see my new doctor that my therapist referred me to.

October 8ᵗʰ 2019

Today was a great day! I spent the day baking and cleaning the house. I finished vacuuming, dusting, sweeping and mopping. I cleaned the whole kitchen and went through the fridge. I was also feeling so energized that I organized the cupboards in the kitchen. I even caught up on laundry. It has been very productive. I am thankful!

October 9ᵗʰ 2019

I am so happy because I've stuck to my new routine since I left the hospital. I wake up around 7:15-7:30am have coffee, wait until about 9:30am and go to the gym for a few hours. After that I usually go to the grocery store and then I cook my meal for the night. I have stuck to a really good diet since I have My Fitness Pal app on my phone which keeps track of my meals. I am working out every day and am hopeful to fit into a small pair of fabletics pants. I have also had therapy and it went great. Missy is happy to see me doing so well and that I am sticking to a routine even if Mitchel is home I still go to the gym. It's different because he has rotating shifts again and mandatory overtime.

October 16ᵗʰ 2019

Today was a fairly good day. It started out OK but as the time passed and I had breakfast and coffee I had to leave for therapy. While at therapy, Kim, my case manager was coming a long too to help understand how things help me and things to do to support me in the future. I began to become "uneasy" which is my code word for paranoid. I was sitting in therapy and the symptoms started up. I was saying, "I'm OK, everything is OK." While doing that I was trying to stop myself at certain times to not go down the "rabbit hole". I was convinced that "They and Them" are coming back now and they slowly plant seeds of deception in my brain. To counter this, we did mindfulness techniques to help calm me down, playdough was used. Like I have said before touch for me is key. After a while of rolling the playdough and describing how it felt and smelt I felt calmer. At the end of the session I was repeating things and talking to myself about my plan going home. I was going to get lunch for Mitchel and I and then head home. I was able to get us lunch, but the drive home was a struggle. I was repeating phrases and images in my mind of being unsafe. I got home and took a PRN Zyprexa like I said I would to my therapist. Tonight, Mitchel works 3-11:00 pm so I'm home alone with my thoughts and symptoms. The Zyprexa made me tired, but I couldn't nap so I sat on the couch doing nothing. As time passed the symptoms got worse. I was calling Bev, my MIL, quite a few times as I struggled with visual hallucinations. Soon that lead into delusional thinking which looking back as I'm writing this is something that I am still convinced would work. I talked about calling the police to come and search my yard for these invisible beings and I thought that if they used an infra-red camera, they would be able to see them, and we could then destroy them. It hit 7:00 pm and it was now med time/bedtime. Mitchel told me to go lay in bed even if I wasn't tired, so I didn't fall asleep in the living room which usually makes things worse because of the windows.

The night passes and soon the next day comes.

October 17ᵗʰ 2019

Another day of feeling uneasy. Mitchel is concerned about my symptoms and worries about me being left alone. I take my Zyprexa again today. It helped a little bit but mainly slowed me down which usually helps bring clarity. I talked to Kim and Rita about my symptoms. They told me to monitor it and see if I need help to contact the help line or family. There wasn't much that would happen with my medication because I had just seen my doctor on Tuesday. Only a couple days of struggles.

October 22ⁿᵈ 2019

Today I am doing really well. After the struggles last week, I am back on track now. Mitchel and I started doing the Ketogenic diet this past Sunday and it has kept me busy with cooking, cleaning, and a lot of dishes. It makes me feel good though to have something that consumes your whole day. I am still going to the gym five times a week while having to manage the household and laundry. I know Mitchel is very thankful for all I have been doing. It makes me think that I can bounce back from short struggles and come back stronger and more understanding of situations. I am hoping for a good end of the year, but we will see. I am also seeing Missy every week still but some weeks she is already full, so I need to get appointments set up ahead of time. But I am still thankful for the medicine that helps me.

October 25ᵗʰ 2019

This will be my last journal entry. I feel like I am in a good place right now with my relationships and my medication. I will continue to have once a week therapy with Missy. Our plan is once I finish the CBT workbook that I have been working on for months we will start into DBT or Dialectical Behavioral Therapy. It is similar to CBT but from what I understand it takes on a large part of mindfulness. I know now that if I stay on my medication there will be no problems. I just have to keep in mind how destructive I can be when it comes to deciding what is best. I always tend to lean toward no medication but, as I have been told by many people that I need it even if I am doing well. I still have to learn to accept my mental illness and all parts that go along with it. As I wrote this book it was like a big reflection into my life and my illness. I know I will talk about not being sick even when I am but I do know one thing, I will always be "OK".

Conclusion on My Journey

Recovery does not mean my illness is gone
Recovery is learning to live with it
Recovery is being able to recognize symptoms

205

Recovery is learning your triggers
Recovery is learning who you are at the core
Recovery takes time
Recovery is tough
Recovery is hard
Recovery is knowing there are bumps in the road
Recovery is thinking on the past
Recovery is making better decisions
Recovery is finding resilience in yourself
Recovery is different for everyone
My recovery is dealing with old problems
My recovery is learning to let go
My recovery is getting to know me
My recovery is realizing my problems
My recovery is getting help
My recovery is medicine for my life
My recovery needs support
My recovery is just beginning.

Epilogue

My last journal entry was on October 25th 2019 and there has been a lot of changes good and bad since then. Money was getting tight between Mitchel and I so he agreed that I could get a job again. I applied at a few places and soon was selected to work at my local pharmacy. The hours were nice only four hours a day Monday through Friday and every other Saturday. I met with my new coworkers and they were very welcoming. While doing the paperwork I was reading the guidelines about medication/drugs at work. I ended up having to ask if it was ok to take PRN medications if needed and I then divulged that I had paranoid schizophrenia and that I may need the medication at times. My boss said that is was fine. As time went on my mental health started to deteriorate and began having symptoms while trying to function at work. While working there I found myself ending up missing work because I had to stay at the crisis facility twice and one hospital in the year of 2020. While I missed work they were understanding but due to mental health I had to leave my position in November of 2020. It had been a hard year with covid and then also many medication changes. Throughout summer of 2020 I tried multiple medications which were: Rexulti, Venlafaxine, Caplyta, and Fanapt. All of these meds had been tried and they were not a success. When it came to November 2020 I had to leave my position at the pharmacy because it wasn't a good fit because of my illness and I was already slacking in my work. 2021 came around and in early spring I stayed at the crisis facility for a while to change medications again. At this time my doctor prescribed risperidone to help but all it did was make me sleep and gain weight. After my discharge a few weeks later, I was hospitalized and was there for three weeks. While at the hospital they did a kind of "drug holiday" where they discontinued some and prescribed new ones. I had discontinued propranolol, Zyprexa, risperidone, and Lamictal and was then prescribed abilify, stelazine, and hydroxyzine. it was a big change but for the better. I was discharged on Mitchel and I's

Anniversary so I was happy to be home for that. Since this hospital stay I was functioning pretty well but then symptoms start to come up again. I thought they were gone but not anymore. In the summer of 2021 my husband had been doing some research on injectable medications and how they work. He wrote my doctor a note about how the medication may not metabolize correctly so he suggested we try injections. My doctor agreed and now prescribed me the injectable version of abilify. I was struggling quite a bit but after the shot I was feeling much better due to the decrease of symptoms. As I am writing this its been three weeks without voices or visions and I continue to do well. I have my next injection at the end of August and am looking forward to the future where I may be able to work again but I have to be well for a few months beforehand.

One other thing that has changed is the relationship with my mother. One weekend my mother and my brothers came down for a visit. It went really well and we had a good time. I began to talk to my mom about mental health and my book that there were things in there that she probably wouldn't like but in the end my mom actually apologized to me about when I was younger and that she couldn't understand what was going on. Although my mom and I have fought in many ways there are still good things that I remember about the time with my mother like when she would joke about my "blondeness" or when she helped stand up for me at school. One memory that I love was watching "Gone with the Wind" and eating Chinese food for my birthday but mainly I'm looking forward to the future of our relationship now that I hope we can heal from the past.

CPSIA information can be obtained
at www.ICGtesting.com
Printed in the USA
BVHW040023261021
619818BV00003B/20